94

COUNTRYSIDE BOOKS
NEWBURY, BERKSHIRE

0112854428

First Published 1994
© Richard Shurey 1994

COUNTRYSIDE BOOKS
3 Catherine Road
Newbury, Berkshire

ISBN 1 85306 315 0

Designed by Mon Mohan
Cover illustration by Colin Doggett
Photographs and maps by the author

Produced through MRM Associates Ltd., Reading
Typeset by Paragon Typesetters, Queensferry, Clwyd
Printed in England

Contents

Publisher's Note

We hope that you obtain considerable enjoyment from this book; great care has been taken in its preparation. However, changes of landlord and actual closures are sadly not uncommon. Likewise, although at the time of publication all routes followed public rights of way or well-established permitted paths, diversion orders can be made and permissions withdrawn.

We cannot accept responsibility for any inaccuracies, but we are anxious that all details covering both pubs and walks are kept up to date, and would therefore welcome information from readers which would be relevant to future editions.

WARWICKSHIRE
Location of the Walks

N

SUTTON COLDFIELD

1 Nether Whitacre
2 Shustoke

BIRMINGHAM

3 Corley Moor

5 Hampton-in-Arden

4 Meriden

COVENTRY

6 Barston

7 Chadwick End

KENILWORTH

RUGBY

8 Tanworth-in-Arden

9 Rowington

10 Hunningham

12 Preston Lowsonford

HENLEY-in-ARDEN

11 Bagot

WARWICK

13 Norton Lindsey

Wootton Wawen 14

Ufton 15

16 Napton-on-the-Hill

Harbury

17

18 Aston Cantlow

STRATFORD-upon-AVON

19 Priors Hardwick

21 Wixford

20 Moreton Morrell

22 Avon Dassett

23 Edgehill

Ilmington

24 Middle Tysoe

25 26

27

Shipston-on-Stour

28 Lower Brailes

29 Cherington

30

Little Compton

Introduction

Warwickshire is known as Shakespeare's county. How appropriate, therefore, that he so loved the inns and taverns around Stratford-upon-Avon. I invite you to travel further afield to the far boundaries of the county to seek out walks around some of my favourite pubs in some magnificent countryside. A little apology for the geographical purists – I have taken the Warwickshire borders to be the historic limits before the poaching of land to form the new, unromantic, West Midlands.

There is a wide variety of countryside in Warwickshire. To the north is the area of the old Forest of Arden, where the soils are less fertile and pockets of the ancient woodlands remain to add charm and interest. The south is the Feldon, with clay and good agricultural lands between the Avon and the limestone uplands. This area is more sparsely populated and over half a million acres are still used for farming. The Cotswolds nudge their way into southern Warwickshire to give perhaps the finest rambling terrain, with the hills climbing to 850 ft above sea level. Here there are the villages of honey-hued stone – and delightfully sited pretty pubs which make fine havens after the exertion of climbing the heights.

Although I have tried to describe the routes as accurately as possible, the countryside is constantly changing. Hedgerows can still be removed, trees felled and stiles and footpath signs obliterated. On the plus side, the County Council has been active of late in rescuing pathways and encouraging greater use of the rights of way network. So take care, and if in doubt ask the locals.

The sketch maps should be sufficient (read with the text of the walk) to follow the routes without difficulty. However, it adds interest to the walk and indicates possible short-cuts if the relevant 1:50 000 Landranger series map is carried.

The car can usually be left in the pub car park whilst doing the walk. However, it is a courtesy to clear this with the landlord.

Children and family parties are now welcomed at most pubs. At many we find such provisions as games rooms, reduced meal portions and garden play areas to burn off surplus energy. However, when there are children in your party please check where children are allowed.

Many of us take our dogs on rambles. I found that my Welsh collie Nell was invariably welcome; although her manners are impeccable she fully understood when the rule was that dogs remain outside.

Richard Shurey
spring 1994

1 Nether Whitacre
The Dog Inn

The Dog is along the leafy Dog Lane and a building has been here since the Domesday survey of 1086. It cannot be this place as the Dog is only some 450 years old. It was most probably once a farm, but now Pat and Stan give a very warm welcome to this M & B house. With masses of brasses and oak wood, it has that comfortable feeling which one expects from a popular country inn. There is an inglenook fireplace and a piano in the lounge. There is also a snug, a dining-room and a bar.

In addition to the regular menu, there is a 'specials' board with a frequent change in the bill of fare. The steak chasseur is a favourite dish and the excellent home-made soup is always popular. Barbecue meals are served during the summer months in the pretty garden. The real ales offered are Bass, Brew XI and Banks's Mild, and the choice of ciders is between draught Strongbow and Taunton Sweet. The Dog is open from 12 noon to 2.30 pm and 6 pm to 11 pm (Monday to Saturday) and 12 noon to 2.30 pm and 7 pm to 10.30 pm (Sunday). Children can join you at lunchtime, if eating, and Nell was on her best behaviour when I visited and was welcomed. The ghost of a lady has been seen here, but Pat confessed that she appears only to visitors.

Telephone: 0675 481318.

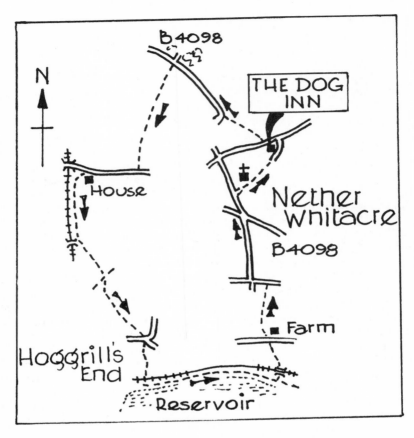

How to get there: Nether Whitacre is on the B4098, about 12 miles east of Birmingham and 3 miles south of Kingsbury. Look for the Dog Inn sign pointing down Dog Lane.

Parking: There is a large car park adjoining the pub.

Length of the walk: 4 miles. Map: OS Landranger series 139 Birmingham and surrounding area (GR 233930).

The pleasant country paths on this walk are gently rural, although within easy reach of Birmingham. Parts of the route are along the waymarked paths of The Heart of England Way and the Centenary Way. The return leg borders Shustoke Reservoir which (besides providing sport for the angler and sailor) supplies Nuneaton and Coventry with water.

The Walk

On entering the lane from the car park, turn left. Within a few steps a path is signed down a vehicle way on the right. At the end enter a sometimes arable field. Follow the arrowed direction (or walk around the edge) to a stile leading to the B4098. Turn right. Within ½ mile and opposite a lane, turn left over a stile. In the field, follow the indicated direction to climb a stile in the opposite boundary. Keep on this heading to a stile leading to a lane.

Turn right. Just before a railway bridge the path is down a vehicle way, left. Past the houses, go left to walk alongside the railway, then, by a footbridge, bear left away from the railway. The path is well marked to a junction of paths. Follow the Heart of England Way arrows to cut off the corner of the field. Bear left at the edge of the arable field. Continue ahead to climb a corner stile into a pasture.

Go diagonally across to a stile, then on to a lane by a junction. Cross to the signed path opposite, which goes around the edge of gardens to a field. Follow the path to a railway. Just beyond is a junction of paths. Turn left. The track borders the reservoir (on the right) and the railway (on the left) for about ¾ mile. Look for a path going left under the railway to a field and bear left to climb out of the vale.

Aim to the left of a farmhouse and climb a stile to a lane. Almost opposite, a path is signed up the bank. Follow the indicated direction, taking great care over the very rough ground. Within a few yards, we are in a pasture. Walk down the field to the stile, midway in the far boundary. Over the stile, walk by a left-hand hedge to a step stile on to a lane. Turn left, then right at the crossroads. At the B4098 turn left. Keep to the right of an inn.

Within 200 yards, turn right down the church drive. Walk through the churchyard, keeping the church on the left. A lane is reached and this leads directly to the Dog Inn.

2 Shustoke
The Plough Inn

The pub building has overlooked the little village green for over 200 years. During this time it has not always been an inn, and was once two farm worker's cottages. During the last war, it housed troops for a while. They no doubt also enjoyed the tranquil countryside around Shustoke.

The Plough is friendly and relaxed; a cosy country pub with a labyrinth of rooms with settles in the corners. All the rooms (inter-connected to the one bar) have old prints, faded framed newspapers, cart wheels and other memorabilia – many things to stimulate interesting conversation. That one bar is well known to knowledgeable beer drinkers, voted local CAMRA Pub of the Year in 1992. It serves Bass, Brew XI and Highgate Mild and a good selection of lagers.

Maurice Quinn and his wife Olivia have been at the Plough for over ten years. Maurice does the cooking as well as helping out alongside Olivia behind the bar. The menu is ideal for ramblers who have worked up an appetite, and the 'toasties', home-cooked ham and home-baked pies are very popular. The lunchtime opening hours are 12 noon to 2.30 pm (Monday to Friday) and 12 noon to 3 pm (Saturday and Sunday). Evening hours are variable. Food is available every day except on Sundays. Children have their own menu, with their favourite beans on toast and chips. Outside, there is a small

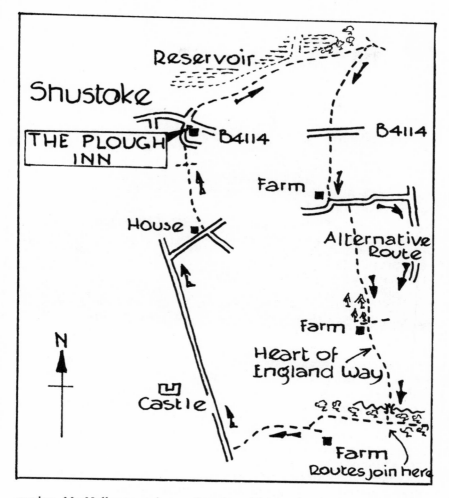

garden. My Nell was welcomed and could join the three dogs who are 'regulars'.

Telephone: 0675 481557.

How to get there: The pub is in the centre of Shustoke on the B4114, just 2 miles east of Coleshill.

Parking: There is a small car park by the pub.

Length of the walk: 5 miles. Map: OS Landranger series 139 Birmingham and surrounding area (GR 227909).

The walk starts on the village green, where there is an ancient animal pound. There is then a lane which borders Shustoke Reservoir (which supplies Coventry) – the waters are used for sailing and fishing. We follow, for a few miles, the route of the Heart of England Way, a long distance footpath stretching from Cannock Chase to the Cotswolds.

The Walk

From the pub cross the road to walk along Bixhill Lane. This becomes a footpath and follows first the edge of fields, then left-hand woods. At the end of the woodlands is a stile and a signed meeting of paths.

Do not climb the stile but retrace a few steps, then cut across the open field, passing an isolated oak to a stile in the far corner (now following the Heart of England Way waymarks). Walk at the right-hand border of the next field to the main road. Cross to the stile opposite.

Follow further waymark arrows and stiles to Moat House Farm. Keep to the left of the farm to gain the lane. Turn left. There are two possible routes over the next stretch.

If you opt to walk over the wide, open fields, which are often cultivated, take the path within 200 yards, signed up a bank. Follow the arrowed direction over the fields, to pick up the side of a wood to a farm drive. Cross directly over. Keep by the right-hand border of the field for 50 yards. When the hedge ends, bear left over the open field. Follow the signed path to drop down the hill, passing an isolated oak to a wood. Here there is a marker post to indicate the direction through the trees to a bridge over a brook. Climb the stile on the far side of the wood. Turn right alongside a right-hand wood.

The alternative is to stay on the lane from Moat House Farm to a T-junction. Turn right to a road junction and take the signed path on the right. The path leads through woods and at the sides of fields to the path alongside the right-hand wood, as above.

At the corner of the woods, climb a stile and bear left in the pasture (with the delightfully named Dumble Farm on the left) to a stile on to the drive. Turn right to a lane and turn right again. We pass the entrance to Maxstoke Castle. This 14th century castle (not open to the public) has often been used in films.

At a junction, turn right along Hollyland. By the next junction (at the far side of a white house on the left), take a signed path. In the field follow the indicated direction, aiming to the left of a distant house. Using stiles, cross a vehicle way. Walk by a right-hand hedge to a corner stile. Continue beside gardens and cut over the grass to a road. Turn left. This road leads back to the Plough Inn.

③ Corley Moor
The Red Lion Inn

The building is about 200 years old and it has been a pub for around half this time. It was previously, I am told, a mortuary and the pub was over the road, where now there is a farmstead and stables. Inside, all is homely, with oak furniture and warm red carpets in the lounge. The bar room is a gem, with stone tile floors that will resist ramblers' boots, a wooden settle that has seated many weary travellers and as the pièce de résistance, a blacked stove and oven in the inglenook.

Pete and Elma Haynes are rightly proud of the food on offer at this house. Pete was a chef for 30 years and prepares most of the food on the premises. The menu is daunting, with the house specialities listed as 'Steak Sizzlers . . . sizzled in our special brandy and oyster sauce with a hint of garlic' and 'River Sizzlers . . . steaks sliced and sizzled in a fiery sweet sauce'. There are at least half a dozen vegetarian dishes available and plenty of 'with chips and beans' meals for the youngsters. There is always a good choice of real ales available, including Bass, Brew XI and Mild. Both Strongbow and Woodpecker cask ciders are available too. The opening hours are 11 am to 'a flexible 3 pm' and 5.30 pm to 11 pm on Monday to Saturday. The Sunday hours are the normal 12 noon to 3 pm and 7 pm to 10.30 pm.

The house dogs (spaniels Bengy and Murphy) do not mind good-mannered friends in the bar (but not, of course, in the lounge or restaurant). Outside, there is plenty of grass and a children's play area. Children are also welcomed to see the goats, sheep and birds, such as pheasants and fantails.

Telephone: 0676 40135.

How to get there: Corley Moor lies east of Birmingham and can be reached from the B4102 Fillongley to Meriden road. Turn along the lane signposted to come to the Red Lion within a mile.

Parking: There are car parks at the front and side of the pub.

Length of the walk: 4 miles. Map: OS Landranger series 140 Leicester and Coventry (GR 275850).

The roar of the motorway is never far away on this route but you will find the charming countryside that inspired the novelist George Eliot over a century ago. The walk is to the village of Fillongley which once boasted two castles, destroyed by Oliver Cromwell.

The Walk

Turn left out of the car park and continue along the lane to the B4102. Turn right to go under the motorway and, 200 yards beyond and by a road junction, turn right through a metal gate.

Walk along a wide vehicle track (once the road). At the end, enter a field through a gate. Turn left along a stony tractor way, following the route of a tiny left-hand brook. When the stony way ends, keep ahead at the side of a field. In a far corner go through a hedge gap and maintain the direction alongside a left-hand hedge.

We pick up another left-hand brook and follow this upstream. Look for an old fence stile on the left, under the branches of a spreading oak tree. Over the stile, cross the brook, using the stepping stones. Now in a pasture, head just to the right of the distant church tower, to a fence stile by a holly bush. Continue in the same direction alongside a right-hand wire fence. To the right are the stones and hummocks where once was one of Fillongley's castles, the moat no doubt being fed from the nearby brook. Walk past one stile (do not climb) to the next, in a corner. Go over the stile and brook and proceed to the street. The interesting church and village are to the left, and a diversion would be worthwhile.

For the walk, turn right for 400 yards, then right again, down Castle Close. Turn left down a vehicle way and continue ahead. In a field pick up the line of a left-hand hedge and pass through a distant corner

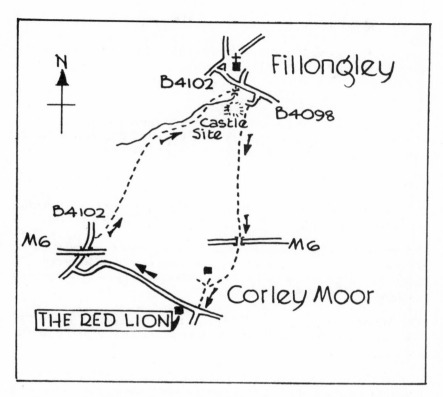

hedge gap. Keep alongside the hedge to another corner gap by a small rivulet. Maintain the direction for a few steps over the open field to a fence stile (which leans at an awkward angle). Follow the arrowed waymark in a pasture and walk the length of the field to go over a fence stile in the distant left-hand corner (another brook is here).

Pick up the line of a right-hand hedge. In a corner (just before a ruined wall), go through a hidden kissing-gate, then another. Climb the bank to a bridge over the motorway. About 20 yards beyond, go left down the bank and through a kissing-gate. There is a winding path through the bushes to Corley Moor. Maintain the direction and keep to the left of a cottage to meet a drive to a lane. The pub is a step or two to the right.

4 Meriden
The Queen's Head

The popularity of this M&B house can be gauged by the longevity of the landlord – Frank Pope has been serving good food and beer here for over twenty-five years. Assisted by Pat in the kitchen he has seen many changes over the years. Earlier landlords had to cope with the demise of business at the end of the stage coach era, this being an important post on the busy coaching route between Birmingham and London, and Frank himself has noted many road changes over the years which have diverted passing trade. He has, however, built up a good reputation and a regular clientele. This is very much a community pub and is renowned for its charity fund-raising efforts.

The Queen's Head is an honest to goodness establishment, offering excellent value for money. The basic menu, which includes a substantial ploughman's, is always supplemented by the 'special of the day'. 'Tiddler' meals are offered for children. The real ales are Bass, Brew XI and Worthington Best Bitter, plus a guest beer. There are draught sweet and dry ciders available. The bars have a friendly ambience with 'no nonsense' floors meant for country feet. On the walls are horse tack and brasses – and you can see what good-looking fellows the Meriden cricket team were in 1908. Outside are children's

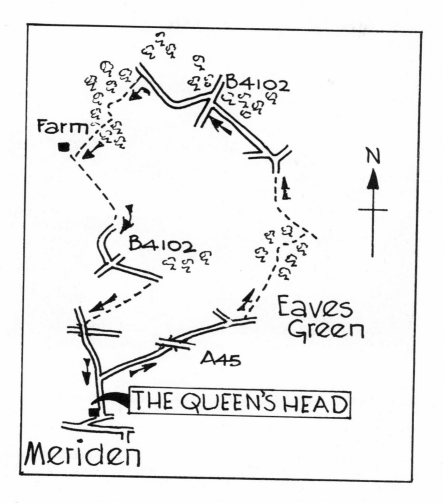

play areas and plenty of benches. Opening hours are from 11 am to 2.30 pm and 5 pm to close (Monday to Saturday) and normal Sunday hours.

Telephone: 0676 22256.

How to get there: Meriden lies east of Birmingham and south of the A45. Take the Coventry road out of Meriden. A mile from the green the inn is signed down a slip road to the left.

Parking: Car parking is available at the side of the pub.

Length of the walk: 4 miles. Map: OS Landranger series 140 Leicester and Coventry (GR 253820).

The pub is in the village that is reputed to be the very centre of England. The countryside around is gently attractive, and this is an ideal autumn walk, as the route passes through some delightful woods.

The Walk

Turn left out of the car park to walk along a lane. Bear right at a junction and pass under the main A45 road. Keep ahead at the next junction at Eaves Green. Just past a mobile homes park, look left for a signed path over a stile which lies back off the road.

We are now on the route of the Heart of England Way. Take the arrowed direction to walk at the edge of a pasture alongside a right-hand hedge. Pass through a corner hedge gap to an area of rough land used for horse jumping. The route is well waymarked to guide us to the very far left corner. Go over a bridge and stile and into woods. There is now a lovely path, twisting this way and that to a stile on to a bridleway.

Turn left, now leaving the Heart of England Way. The bridleway becomes a vehicle way then a lane. At a T-junction, turn left, then keep ahead at a junction to walk along Beck's Lane. At the B4102, turn right, then immediately left along Kinwalsey Lane.

Within ⅓ mile and just before a wood, turn left over a stile. Walk at the border of the right-hand woodlands. In a corner, climb a rough fence stile and maintain the direction by the wood. Follow the edge of the field around bends to a new step stile into the woods. Keep ahead along a well-worn track, going over crossing paths to a stile into an arable field. Cross the open field, aiming to the left of the farmhouse, to meet a farm vehicle track.

Turn left to pass a ruined wind pump. The track becomes a lane to the B4102. Cross to the opposite lane. Within 400 yards, climb a stile on the right. After 30 yards, strike out over the open field. A line of isolated trees shows the route to a distant stile. Walk over piles of discarded roadstone to a lane. Turn left to cross a bridge over the A45. The lane leads to the Queen's Head.

5 Hampton-in-Arden
The White Lion

'Ay now I am in Arden the more fool I,' said Touchstone in *As You Like It*. Not true, for in the old Forest of Arden is some gentle, delightful countryside and this pub is a welcoming hostelry. There was an inn mentioned in Domesday (1086) as being opposite the church in Hampton. Whether this was on exactly the same site as the White Lion, the licensee of the Mitchells and Butlers house could not say. Records do verify, however, that good ale and food has been offered here for 400 years.

The two front bars are the Lion's Den and Daniel's Bar. The latter I found a gem of a place – a dozen drinkers and it is packed. Dog Nell was allowed to join me, though. A fixed wooden settle and a bench have perhaps not been in place for all the 400 years, but certainly a great many of them. There is more comfort in the larger bar and at the rear is a modern restaurant. The meals are all home-made and very appetising. The steaks are renowned but I like the sound of the Spicy Barbecue Platter, made up of minted lamb chop, spare rib and chicken. Children can have half portions and there is also a children's menu. Vegetarians too, are well catered for. The selection of beers is Brew XI, Bass and a guest. There is a small grassed area with benches

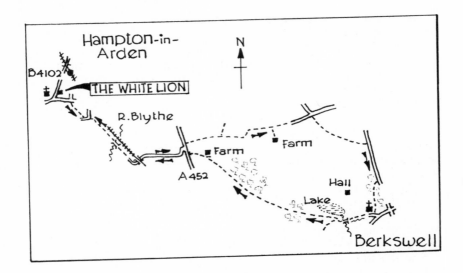

and tables and the front of the building also serves as the village notice board, with a host of activities advertised. The hours of opening are 12 noon to 2.30 pm and 5 pm to 11 pm (Monday to Thursday) and all day Friday and Saturday. Sunday has the usual restricted hours. Telephone: 0675 442833.

How to get there: Hampton-in-Arden is midway between Solihull and Meriden on the B4102. The White Lion is on the edge of the village, opposite the church.

Parking: The car park is off the B4102 at the rear of the pub.

Length of the walk: 6 miles. Map: OS Landranger series 139 Birmingham and surrounding area (GR 204808).

Early on the walk the route crosses the little river Blythe, over a 500 year old packhorse bridge. Over the main road is quiet countryside before the halfway village of Berkswell. Here there is a wealth of fascinating things, including the ancient well where monks were baptised, the stocks (with five holes to accommodate a one-legged offender with his companions), a little museum, and the interesting church. The return section goes alongside a wood which is scented by bluebells in springtime.

The Walk
From the car park, turn left on the B4102. Almost at once, turn left again down Marsh Lane. Within ¼ mile and opposite Elm Tree Close,

go over a stile by a gate on the right. Walk down the elongated pasture to a stile in the far left corner. At once, climb another stile to a cul-de-sac road. Turn left for a few steps. As the road twists sharp left, the path is signed ahead along a house drive. Keep ahead to climb a stile, then walk alongside a fence to a stile into a pasture. Maintain the direction to a stile by a gate into an often sown field. The heading is arrowed to follow a route gradually nearing the railway embankment on the left.

Follow the way, going over the packhorse bridge, then joining a vehicle way and lane. Follow the lane left under the railway and continue along it to the main A452 road. Almost opposite, a bridleway is signed along a 'private' farm road.

Keep on the farm road, passing the farm drive, and continue to a junction. The next path is signed through a gate on the right. Take the direction indicated to cross the field to a stile in the opposite hedge. Maintain the heading over a pasture to drop down to the far left corner. Climb a stile by a gate (dog flap for your Fido and my Nell), but watch the mud.

Continue for a few yards alongside a right-hand wire fence, then maintain the direction to the next stile in a hedge. Beyond, walk near a right-hand hedge to a fence stile by a gate to the left of a white cottage. Turn right on the road.

Just before houses on the left, pass through a kissing-gate on the right. Walk a few steps through the trees to a pasture. Walk by the left-hand border, with the elegant 18th century Berkswell Hall away to the right. Go along the edge of the churchyard to a road at Berkswell. Turn right through the church gate and continue alongside a wall, keeping the church on your right.

Maintain the direction, passing through two kissing-gates into a pasture and along a wooden causeway above a stream. Go over a bridge and walk through a wood. There is a kissing-gate onto a cart track. Cross straight over, along a path signed to Hampton. The path is well trodden over an open field to a distant stile. Beyond, walk at the borders of woods and fields. Go over a stile to pastureland and keep the heading to a farmstead. On the drive, turn left to the main road. Cross to rejoin the outward route and retrace your steps to Hampton and the White Lion.

6 **Barston**
The Bull's Head

The Bull's Head is a listed building with a history going back to 1490. There is even a priest hiding-hole upstairs. The quiet lane outside was once the main coaching route between Coventry and Birmingham and the inn, at that time, provided overnight accommodation and had many stables at the rear.

This is a typical village pub. If you want loud pop music and fruit machines this is not the place for you. But if you want cosy bars and good food and ale, mine hosts Martin and Joy Bradley will give you a warm welcome.

There are two bars, but of especial interest to the many parties of walkers is the small dining place at the rear, where the old timbers in the walls and ceilings make this a unique room full of atmosphere of days long past. There is a wide variety of wall furnishings that will stimulate much conversation, including several old newspapers which have been framed. I enquired about the availability of one of the products advertised in 1930 – Kruschen Salts (price 6d) which are guaranteed to remove the aches of rheumatism within two weeks. Alternatively, there is an AJS motor cycle for £39.

The food is traditional pub fare, much of it home-cooked, with a particularly interesting range of sandwiches. The opening hours are the usual times and food is available every day except Sunday. The real ales served are well-kept Bass and Brew XI. The resident dogs welcome the companions of regular customers so probably Fido will find a friend (but not in the food areas, of course). For warmer days, there are plenty of tables and benches in the gardens to the rear and side of the pub.

Telephone: 0675 442830.

How to get there: Barston lies south-east of Solihull. Approaching from the B4102 Henley-in-Arden road, turn just by a canal bridge, 1 mile from Solihull. Barston is reached after 3 miles. The Bull's Head is on the left at the start of the village.

Parking: There is a car park at the rear.

Length of the walk: 4 miles. Map: OS Landranger series 139 Birmingham and surrounding area (GR 207781).

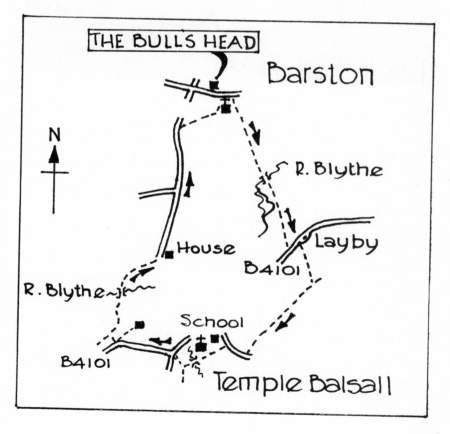

The first mile or so is over farmland (crossing the little river Blythe) on the way to Temple Balsall. The land here was given to the Knights Templar (who protected pilgrims to the Holy Land) in 1150. There is a historic church and elegant almshouses, dated late 17th century, clustered around a broad courtyard and an ancient refectory. On the return the 19th century Springfield House (now a school) is passed.

The Walk

On the lane from the car park turn left, then almost at once right, through the main church gates (with a lantern above) to the church-yard of Barston's St Swithin's church, built of small bricks in 1721. Keeping to the left of the building, continue to the stile into a pasture. Follow the clear path to another stile onto often arable lands.

Keep ahead, walking with a hedge on the right-hand side. In a far corner go through a hedge gap and, keeping in the same direction, walk over the open field to a bridge over the river Blythe. We are now in a large arable field. Keep by the right-hand border for about 300 yards, then strike out over the open field. There are few landmarks but, if the route is not worn by feet, aim to the left of distant electricity pylons.

Climb a stile onto the B4101 and turn left for 100 yards. Just before a layby, turn right over a rather hidden stile. Follow the left-hand edge of the field. In a far corner go under a fence bar to a junction of paths. Turn right, with a hedge on the right, to a road. Turn right.

Just before a school, turn left along a path signed to the church, to pass the almshouses. Follow the path over a brook to the gates of a cemetery. Turn right through a kissing-gate. The path through the woods divides. Take the left-hand fork to a lane. Turn right, then at once left along the B4101. Immediately past the drive to Springfield House, take a path on the right (the sign may be broken or missing). Through the trees a drive is reached. Turn right. Just before buildings, turn left along a hedged way to a vehicle way. Follow this for a few yards, with school buildings nearby, then bear left along a track through trees and bushes.

Emerging on a meadow through a kissing-gate, continue through gates to cross the once elegant bridge over the river. Join a tractor way which veers right. Go over a stile beside a gate and continue along the way of tractors to a stile on to a lane. Note the nearby house built 'Circa Queen Anne 1664–1714'. Walk along the lane and keep ahead at a junction. Within another ⅓ mile, take a signed path over a stile to the right. Walk up the pasture to the fence stile between two trees. Continue in the next pasture near the left-hand border to a hidden stile in the far left-hand corner. This leads to the churchyard at Barston again, then the lane. The Bull's Head is to the left.

⑦ Chadwick End
The Orange Tree

This pub is part of the Whitbread Brewer's Fayre chain. It combines the cosiness of the country hostelry of the past (the building is 17th century) with the undoubted value for money of a large organisation. Families especially are encouraged. There are plenty of corners in the bars for quite conversation and if the talk drags there are many interesting items decorating the walls, including cases of old cigarette cards and postage stamps, paintings and prints and stuffed wild birds.

The range of food is very reasonably priced, with the duck in an orange sauce being very popular. Vegetarian meals are always available and specials of the day are listed on the colourful blackboard behind the bar. Children are catered for with their own menu. There is a family dining-room and, besides the outdoor play area, an indoor games room. No dogs at this pub, I'm afraid. The beers on offer are Boddingtons, Wadworth 6X and Flowers Original, and for cider drinkers the choice is between sweet and dry Woodpecker and Strongbow. The pub is open all day.

Telephone: 0564 782458.

How to get there: Chadwick End is midway between Warwick and Solihull on the A4141. The Orange Tree is in the middle of the hamlet.

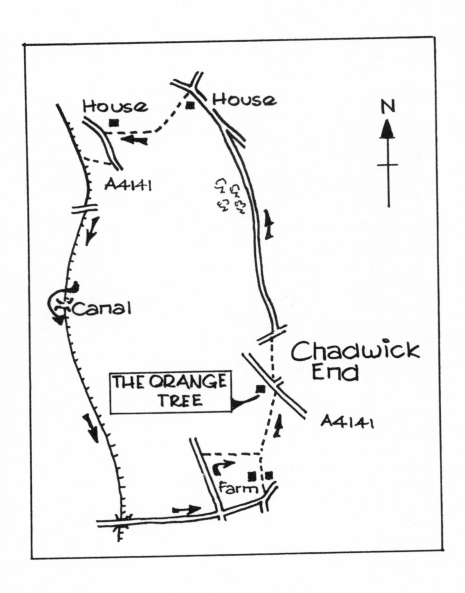

Parking: There is a car park at the front of the pub.

Length of the walk: 5 miles. Map: OS Landranger series 139 Birmingham and surrounding area (GR 207731).

The walk starts with a mile or so along lovely winding lanes, then there is a view of Chadwick Manor which was built for a manufacturer of soap in 1875. The towpath of the Grand Union Canal is used on the return leg.

The Walk

From the car park, take care while crossing the busy road. Between the post box and phone box, follow the line of stepping stones in the grass – this marks the way to a footpath. Walk at the rear of the gardens of bungalows. The going may be a little overgrown for a yard or two but the track ends at a stile to an arable field. Walk alongside the left-hand hedge to a far metal gate on to a lane. Turn right, then at once left along Chadwick Lane. This is a fine narrow highway.

Keep ahead at a junction. Within 400 yards (and by another road junction at Park Corner), turn left. The path is signed down a house drive. Keep to the right of the White House on the well used track. Pass through a gate to a farm track and go right to pass over a brook.

The main track bends right to barns but we maintain the old direction, walking towards a fine house. The path is signed to keep to the left of the garden and house. Pass through a little gate to the main road and turn left for 300 yards. Take a vehicle way, on the right, which leads to an inn and the Grand Union Canal. Turn left along the towing path with the water on your right. Stay by the waterway for about 2 miles, with the towing path crossing to the other bank at a bridge.

At a road bridge, numbered '66', leave the canal. Gain the road and turn right to cross the water. At the road junction (with the drive to Baddesley Clinton Hall to the right) you have a choice of two routes.

One possibility is to walk straight on at the junction, and take a path signed left down the drive of Convent Farm. This avoids a short section on the main route which may be a little muddy and difficult.

For the main walk, turn left at the road junction and continue for a little under ½ mile. Turn right through an old kissing-gate beside a rough metal gate and follow the farm cart track. When this turns left into a field, maintain the old direction, ignoring the rather confusing waymark arrow. Passing a barrier, follow the clear path through bushes and trees. Pick up the edge of a left-hand pool and continue through the short, possibly boggy, section. Climb a rough fence stile and walk along a wide green way with a hedge to the left and a row of trees to the right. In a corner climb a fence stile and go over a plank bridge. Turn left (barns to the right) to pass through a rough metal gate. The diversion joins the main route here.

Walk by a right-hand wide ditch to go through a gate into a ridged pasture. Proceed alongside a right-hand border to climb a rough corner stile. Follow the arrowed directions to continue to a step stile to the main road. The Orange Tree is a few steps to the left.

8 Tanworth-in-Arden
The Bell Inn

Tanworth-in-Arden is a pretty village and the Bell is a traditional rural pub, overlooking the trim green with its typical spreading chestnut tree. There is nothing fancy about the Bell – it provides a pleasant, friendly haven with simple but wholesome fare after a walk through the lands of Arden. Here you can see notices about horse shows, gymkhanas and flower shows – and there is a rather forbidding list of punishments (such as a fine of £2.2s.0d for 'stealing wick, yarn and cloth laid out to whiten') administered by the Tanworth Association for the prosecution of felons. Stephen Carter now holds the licence but locals still talk with pride of the 30 years when 'mine host' was Jack Hood, the celebrated boxer who won a Lonsdale Belt in 1926.

The Bell Inn offers typical pub fare, with its gammon being particularly recommended. The real ales are Boddingtons, Wadworth 6X and IPA. It is a particular pleasure in the summer months to take a pint outside on the green. By the way, Fido can join you here, or in the bar, but not in the lounge. Opening hours are from 11 am to 11 pm, with meals available from 12 noon to 2 pm and 7 pm to 9 pm. Normal Sunday hours apply.

Telephone: 056 44 2212.

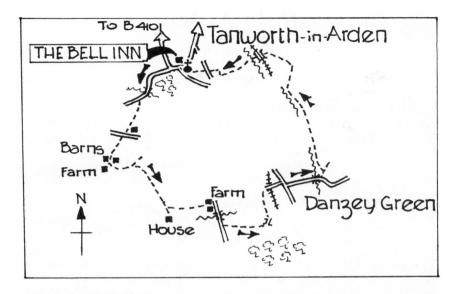

How to get there: Tanworth-in-Arden lies south-west of Solihull and is reached along lanes, about 1 mile off the B4101. The pub is on the green in the centre of the village.

Parking: There is a large car park behind the pub.

Length of the walk: 4 miles. Map: OS Landranger series 139 Birmingham and surrounding area (GR 117706).

There is not much of the ancient Forest of Arden left, but this is an attractive area of a gentle rolling pastoral countryside. The last mile or so of the walk is along the valley of the infant river Alne. The paths are well waymarked.

The Walk

Out of the car park, turn right to walk along the picturesque main street of Tanworth. We pass cottages with pretty gardens and the village shop. As the road twists sharp right, turn left along Brown's Lane. Walk past the Whitehead Almshouses, which are dated 1871. Continue around a bend, then the lane drops downhill to cross a hidden brook. A few steps further, climb a stile on the left. In the field walk alongside the left-hand hedge, then to the right of a large barn to a lane.

Turn right, then at once left over a fence stile. Continue at the side of a field towards a farmstead. Go through a rough metal railing gate.

Walk between barns (rather muddy) to the vehicle way by the farmhouse. Turn left. Past entrances to houses, turn right over a cattle grid, signed as a footpath. The vehicle driveway drops down to another cattle grid. Stay on the drive, passing a pool. Just before the gate to the house, turn left alongside the wooden fence to a corner stile. Cross a footbridge. Here two paths are signed. We keep ahead alongside a left-hand wire fence.

At a farm, walk between barns and to the left of the farmhouse to a lane. Turn right to go over a brook. Just beyond, a footpath is signed on the left. In the field, walk past a barn and, at the left-hand edge of the field, continue to a step stile. Keep at the border of a right-hand wood. Take care now. Go past a hunting gate and stay by the edge of woodlands.

Follow the line of a wire fence by the woods, passing an abandoned lorry. Cross a brook to a step stile to a pasture and take the direction indicated by a waymark arrow. Continue to a stile. Over this, go across a new bridge spanning a stream. A wide farm track goes over a railway bridge to a road. Turn right, then at once left along a lane. Within ¼ mile, the lane twists sharp right by a house called Half Acre.

Take the left-hand signed path to pass a bungalow. About 200 yards along the vehicle drive take a signed path over a stile to the left. Continue to follow waymarks, with the little river Alne on the left. When the way is divided by waymark arrows at a distant stile, take the right-hand fork to climb another stile by a dead tree trunk. Cross the water here.

Walk the length of a long pasture. Pass under electricity lines to a far stile by a field gate. Follow the path, passing under the railway, and continue across the pasture to a bridge, to cross the little river. Follow the left-hand border of the field beyond, to walk around corners to a waymarked step stile. The arrows lead us to a lane. Turn right, then at once left. The path leads to the church at Tanworth-in-Arden. Walk through the churchyard to the green and the Bell Inn.

Rowington
The Tom o' the Wood

There is a windmill on the sign of this 17th century canalside Whitbread house and I asked Geoff Harvey, one of the joint licensees, about the story behind the name. Tom owned the sawmill at the hamlet at nearby Finwood. He was a local character and the windmill was called after him. This gave the name to the pub, which had previously been the Old New Inn.

The Tom o' the Wood has a wide range of appetising meals on the menu and many ramblers do justice to the massive mixed grill. Above the pub is a restaurant – Stones. The name is appropriate as the feature is that meals are placed on individual stones and popped in the oven. Children are well catered for, with especial favourites being the pizzas and beefburgers and chips. The real ales offered are Boddingtons, Morland Old Speckled Hen, Flowers and Marston's. The landlord is particularly proud of the condition of his Newcastle Brown. Ciders include Woodpecker and Red Rock. There are plenty of benches and tables in the pretty gardens, to be enjoyed when the weather permits. My Nell (and other dogs) are asked to remain outside.

Telephone: 0564 782252.

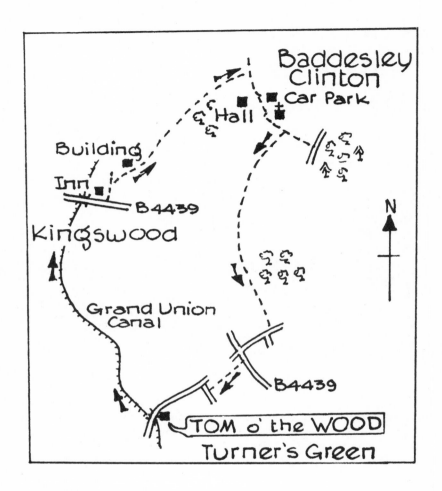

How to get there: Rowington itself lies on the B4439. Approaching from Hockley Heath, go over two canal bridges. One mile further, turn right at a crossroads. The pub is on the left, ½ mile along the lane.

Parking: There is a car park alongside the Tom o' the Wood.

Length of the walk: 4 miles. Map: OS Landranger series 139 Birmingham and surrounding area (GR 195697).

The walk starts along the Grand Union Canal, which was formed by amalgamating a number of waterways to link the Midlands with London. A magnificent moated manor house is visited. Baddesley Clinton dates from medieval times and is now in the care of the National Trust.

The Walk

From the car park, walk a few steps to the canal. Cross the water and at once drop down left to the towing path. Turn left to pass under the lane, with the canal now on your right side. At the next road bridge, go up steps to gain the road. Turn right to walk along the B4439, passing another inn. Within about 200 yards, turn left down a vehicle track (signed as a footpath). Go over a stile by a gate and pass to the right of a large brick building. Go through a gate and take the arrowed direction, passing under high electricity lines.

Continue to the far corner and climb a stile. Maintain the heading, picking up the side of the grounds of Baddesley Clinton. This lovely 15th century house has changed little since 1634. Here you can see priests' secret hiding places, family portraits, the old chapel and lovely gardens. Open March to October, afternoons only, Wednesday to Sunday inclusive and on bank holiday Monday afternoons. Continue to the vehicle drive. Turn right. Follow the route for cars but do not turn into the car parking area. Continue, instead, to the entrance of the house. Turn left along a footpath, signed to the church. We are now on the long-distance footpath of the Heart of England Way.

Walk along the tree-lined path to Baddesley Clinton church. The tower of the lovely building was constructed about 1500 by Nicholas Brome in remorse for having killed a priest. Follow the path through the churchyard to the drive.

Turn right to walk along a fenced track at the side of sheep pastures. Keep on the waymarked path to a lane. Turn right, then left at the B4439. Within a few steps, take a signed path on the right which leads to a lane. Continue right, to a T-junction. Turn left. The Tom o' the Wood is ¼ mile along the lane.

⑩ Hunningham
The Red Lion

The Red Lion is alongside the 14th century bridge (protected by English Heritage) across the tranquil river Leam, along which the pub has fishing rights. The building was probably a coaching inn at the river crossing and dates from the 16th century. This is another of those unpretentious rural English pubs which makes exiles in far off lands sigh for their homeland. There is nothing grand about this free-house, run by John and Shirley Hill, where darts and dominoes are played, but, in addition to a friendly welcome, you will find good ale and a menu of traditional inn food at reasonable prices.

The list of available (food on a standard menu and a 'specials' blackboard) represents excellent value. I especially recommend the fish dishes – locally caught trout and escalope of salmon in a cucumber and dill sauce – and my favourite forbidden 'pud', spotted dick with lashings of custard. There is always a vegetarian dish available and barbecues in the summer months. The well-kept real ales are M&B Brew XI, Bass, Theakston XB and Mansfield Old Bailey. Strongbow and Scrumpy Jack ciders are also available. There is an extensive garden with plenty of tables and benches in an old orchard. Alongside is a Caravan Club 'listed' site. There are plenty of grassy

areas where children can use up their surplus energy after the ramble. If it is not 'garden weather', there is a special family room. The opening hours are 12 noon to 3 pm and 6.30 pm to 11 pm daily (with normal Sunday hours applicable).
Telephone: 0926 632715.

How to get there: Hunningham lies 4 miles east of Leamington Spa and is signed from the B4453. The Red Lion is just over the bridge across the river Leam.

Parking: There is a large car park alongside the inn.

Length of the walk: 4 miles. Map: OS Landranger series 151 Stratford-upon-Avon and surrounding area (GR 373686).

The walk is along the valley of the meandering little river Leam, a tributary of the Avon. We pass the humble Norman church at Hunningham. There is another old church at Wappenbury where the tower has been looking out over the green watermeadows since the 15th century.

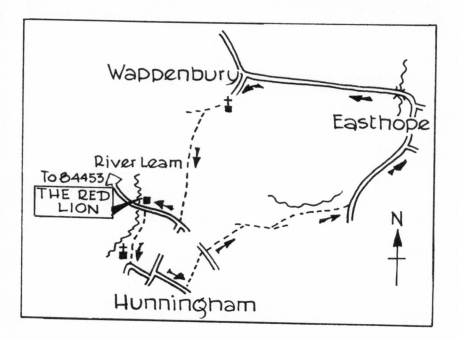

The Walk

From the car park, cross the road to climb over a stile. Take the direction of the signed path and go over a further stile. At the end of the second meadow, climb the bank on the left to go over the stile at the top of the bank. Follow the fence to the right for 70 yards to climb another stile, back to the riverside. Turn left to a stile into a meadow.

Bear 45° left to walk to the left of the church. Follow the edge of the churchyard to a stile. On the lane, turn left to a road. Turn left, then at once right, along a lane. Within 400 yards, take a signed path up the bank to the left. In the field, keep by the right-hand border to the far corner. Walk between wire fences (watch out for stinging nettles in summer), then go through a little gate. At a road go a few steps right, then climb a stile on the left. In the pasture take the arrowed direction to a stile in the opposite boundary.

Maintain the direction to a far stile onto a cart track. This stile was erected in memory of Bill Challenor, an official of Leamington Rambling Club for many years. Turn right. Within 400 yards, take a path bearing off left. The path direction is indicated to just 'nudge' the river Leam.

Go over a distant stile beside a metal gate. Walk beside the left-hand border of a field to a hidden corner double stile. Follow the indicated direction to a stile onto a lane. Turn left, then bear left at a junction to pass a pretty thatched cottage. Keep ahead, following the lane over the bridge by the weir. A lovely spot this, with a seat to rest awhile.

Follow the road to Wappenbury and take the cul-de-sac lane, left, to the church. Bear to the right of the church, then at once go right again along a wide stony track, signed as a bridleway. Walk past a white building. Within 300 yards there is a division of ways. Go left through a bridlegate. Follow the clear track to cross the river over a bridge. Keep ahead over a pasture, then pass through a bridlegate into a sown field. Keep at the edge and continue along the bridleway to the road. The Red Lion is to the right.

⑪ Preston Bagot
The Crab Mill

The name of the pub does not refer to seaside crabs but to the wild apples which once grew so profusely in the countryside. Sadly, crab apple trees seem to be a lot rarer these days, with so many hedgerows being grubbed out. We can see on the rather fine sign how the fruit was crushed to make cider and preserves in past days. The building was once an inn for agricultural workers and there are some fascinating prints on the walls of the stone-flagged bar of former rural scenes, such as the steam-powered threshing machine and the women on their knees picking the potato crop.

The Crab Mill is one of the few pubs that, in these more enlightened days, stays open all day. The Whitbread managed house provides meals and drinks when you want them, so that you do not have to carefully time your walk to ensure refreshments at the end. There is a wide selection of real ales, including Flowers Original, Wadworth 6X and Boddingtons. Draught and bottled ciders are also available. The menu is extensive, with vegetarians especially well catered for. 'Specials' of the day are chalked on a board behind the bar. This is a family pub and I especially like the welcome to youngsters. They not only have their own Charlie Chalk menu (chips with everything, of course) but also their own room in which to eat their favourite meals.

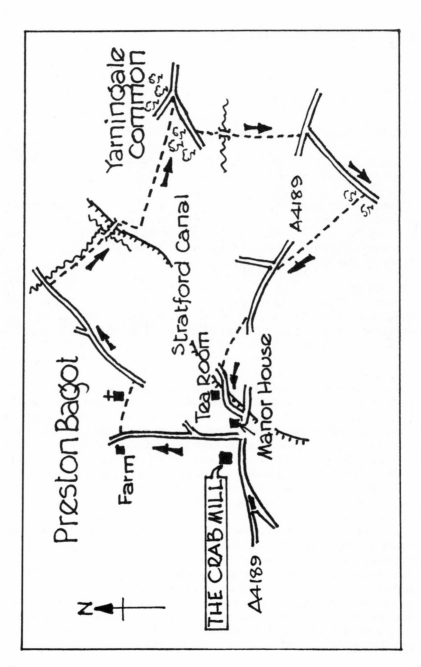

There is a play area outside the Crab Mill. I think it best if Fido is kept outside.

Telephone: 0926 843342.

How to get there: The Crab Mill is 1 ½ miles from Henley-in-Arden, on the A4189 Warwick road.

Parking: There is a large car park in front of the pub.

Length of the walk: 3 miles. Map: OS Landranger series 151 Stratford-upon-Avon and surrounding area (GR 172653).

There are some magnificent pathways in this pastoral countryside. The walk goes to Yarningale Common – one of the few commons remaining in Warwickshire – and crosses the Stratford Canal, which was completed in 1816 to convey coal southwards and corn and lime in the opposite direction. The waterway was restored by the National Trust in recent years.

The Walk
Turn left out of the car park to walk along the A4189. Within a few steps, take the lane on the left. Keep ahead at a junction. Almost opposite a farm, take a footpath on the right. Climb the hill (passing a seat) to the Norman church of All Saints, Preston Bagot. The trim building has a shingled bell turret. Continue, with the church on the left, to a lane. Turn left.

Take the right-hand fork at a Y-junction and drop down the hill. Immediately before a brook, take a signed path on the right. In the pasture, keep near the left-hand brook to meet the canal. Cross the water over the bridge – note the slit down the middle of the bridge which meant the canal bargees did not have to unhitch their horses.

In the opposite field, bear right to the far left corner. Turn left to walk beside a left-hand hedge. Continue on the same heading, to join a vehicle way to a lane at Yarningale Common. Turn right. Within ¼ mile, a path is signed on the left. Walk a few yards through the trees to a step-stile.

Continue along a fenced way to climb another stile. Maintain the heading over a brook and continue to the A4189. Cross to the opposite lane. A path is indicated on the right after ½ mile. The way is a little muddy and overgrown to a stile into a pasture. Walk by a right-hand wire fence. Climb the stile on the top of the rise. Follow the arrowed heading to the A4189 again. Turn left. After 300 yards, take the obsolete road on the right as far as the canal – a tearoom is here. Follow the lane to the A4189. Turn right to the Crab Mill, passing (on the right) the 16th century timbered manor house.

12 **Lowsonford**
The Fleur de Lys

The 17th century Fleur de Lys, which was originally a row of cottages, is full of atmosphere, having ceilings thick with low beams, and up and down stone and tile floors, worn by the feet of countless customers over the centuries. There are many heavy timber roof supports, which means there are hidden alcoves for that cosy tête à tête. The oak furniture enhances the friendly feel and there are three open fires in wintertime.

For the last few decades, the inn has been synonymous with pies. In the 1950s Mr Brookes who was then the landlord started making and selling hot chicken and mushroom pies with peas. In those far off days meals in pubs were rarities – one was lucky to get a rather ancient sandwich or a packet of plain crisps – and the fame of the lovely pies spread far and wide. Today pies (in at least three varieties) are still made in this delightful old canalside pub but, in addition, many other delectable dishes (but definitely no sandwiches) are available. The frequently changed bill of fare is decoratively chalked on a huge board and some vegetarian meals are always included. The pub is one of Whitbread's Wayside Inns and Russell Proctor and Tim Woodcock (the joint licensees) ensure the smooth running. The large range of real

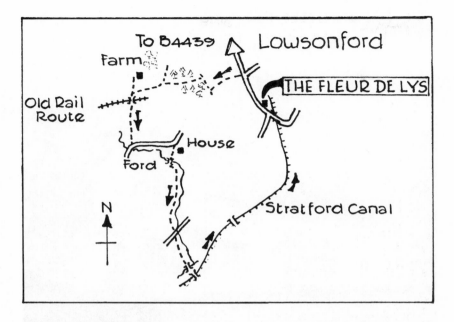

ales makes a choice difficult. You can choose from Wadworth 6X, Boddingtons Bitter and Mild, Marston's Pedigree, Wethered Winter Royal and Flowers Original. In addition to bottled cider, there is draught Strongbow.

There are magnificent lawns, where willows dip low into the canal, and plenty of benches and tables which Fido is allowed to guard as he is not allowed into the pub. Children have their play area, with magnificent contraptions on which to climb. There is also a galleried family room which is said to be haunted. Youngsters will soon find the toy cupboard after they have selected from their own menu – chips with everything of course but healthy fresh vegetables as well. The pub is open all day, every day (although there are some restrictions on drinking hours for alcoholic drinks).

Telephone: 0564 782431.

How to get there: Lowsonford is signposted from the B4439 Warwick road, about 2 miles from Hockley Heath.

Parking: There is a large car park to the rear of the pub.

Length of the walk: 4 miles. Map: OS Landranger series 151 Stratford-upon-Avon and surrounding area (GR 188678).

The first footpaths are along the long-distance path, the Heart of England Way. The route is through a landscape of gentle woods and fields which were once part of the vast Forest of Arden. The return to the pub is alongside the Stratford Canal, which was constructed in 1816.

Some sections of this walk are very muddy at times — wear wellies or strong boots.

The Walk

Out of the car park, turn right along the lane. At a road junction in the centre of the village, turn left by a phone box and walk along a vehicle track. By the cottage at the far end, climb a stile into a pasture. Follow the direction indicated to climb another stile. The path beyond is clear to a cart track. Turn right to cross what was once a bridge over a railway.

Continue to a signed junction of paths. Climb a stile, then at once another, to go 90° left. Walk at the side of an arable field alongside a left-hand wood. Go over a corner stile to enter woods. Follow the clear track through the trees to a pasture. Follow the arrowed way right, to a farm tractor way. Turn left through a metal gate. The tractor way then bends right. Follow this to a stile on to a farm 'road'. Turn left to again cross the old rail route (affectionately known as the 'Coffeepot Line'). Follow the road to a lane. Turn left. Within ⅓ mile, the lane twists sharp left. Go right, down a vehicle way, passing a new barn conversion.

We come to a ford. There is a footbridge for walkers, but it is not quite long enough, so you may have to use stepping stones to reach the start. Safely over the water, continue along the vehicle way for a further 20 yards. Turn left to take a signed path over a stile.

The path now hugs a left-hand brook through pastures. Keep the water on your left to a stile on to a lane. Cross and climb the stile opposite. Again, keep by the left-hand brook through meadows, to pass through a far white metal gate. The track beyond is often muddy as it nears the canal. Turn left along the towing path. Pass a cottage and an aqueduct where the waterway passes over a stream. At a lock, the towing path crosses to the opposite bank. Note the slit down the bridge which obviated the need for the towing ropes to be unhitched when horses pulled the barges.

Stay on the towing path, passing a nature reserve, to a road bridge (numbered '41'). Just before, go through the gate on the right, onto a lane. Turn left to go over the canal. At a junction, bear right. The Fleur de Lys is along the lane on the right.

Norton Lindsey
13 The New Inn

In the middle of the 19th century there were three inns in the village, serving the agricultural community. Besides the New Inn, which opened around 1810, there was the Old Red Horse (once called the Crown) and next door (and rather confusingly) the Red Horse. The New Inn was owned by the Mann family who were farmers and also acted as slaughterers. By 1970 there was only one pub – the New Inn. The present building was constructed in the mid 1930s (one brick width around the original building) by Mr Strong, a Birmingham builder. The architecture outside is therefore typical of that period, while inside some attempt has been made to retain an older style.

John and Rosemary Tranter have been at the New Inn (owned by Enterprise Taverns) for over eight years and provide old-fashioned hospitality. Brew XI and Bass real ales are offered and there is a modest but excellent-value food menu. The home-made steak and mushroom pie and the lasagne are very popular, as is the ham off the bone. A 'Special of the Day' is listed in the menu and our vegetarian friends can always find a suitable appetising dish. Children's portions are available, but – sorry Nell and Fido – dogs are not welcomed. There is a neat garden at the rear, with plenty of benches and tables. Opening

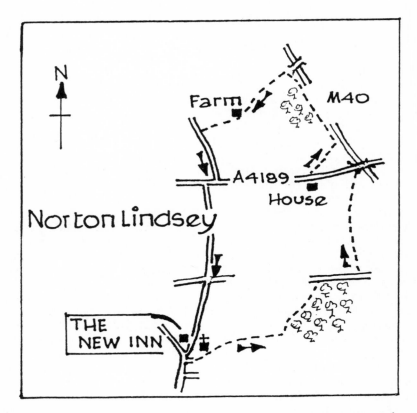

hours (meal times a little shorter) are from 11 am to 2.30 pm and 6 pm to 11 pm (Monday to Saturday) and the usual 12 noon to 3 pm and 7 pm to 10.30 pm on Sunday.
Telephone: 0926 842303.

How to get there: Norton Lindsey is signed from the A4189 Henley road, 4 miles west of Warwick. The New Inn is on the south side of the village.

Parking: A car park is at the side of the pub.

Length of the walk: 3 miles. Map: OS Landranger series 151 Stratford-upon-Avon and surrounding area (GR 228631).

The walk is over undulating farmland with several small woods to add variety. The area was a lot quieter before the M40 came, but we soon escape from the noise.

Towards the end of the route a derelict windmill (sadly without its sails) can be seen. It was built in 1795 and last worked in 1906.

The Walk

Go out of the front exit of the car park and turn left. Main Street becomes Snitterfield Lane. Within a step or two, turn left down Church Road to the church. The original church, consisting of the present nave only, was built in 1220. Walk through the churchyard, keeping the building on your left side, to pass through the metal kissing-gate in the far left-hand corner. Continue at the side of an often sown field, walking by a left-hand hedge. In a corner, turn left over a plank bridge. Follow the bottom edge of the field with woodlands on the right-hand side.

Through a corner gap, maintain the heading to a stile on to a lane. Turn right for 300 yards. Turn left along the bridleway signed through a gate. Walk beside the hedge, then pass through a corner gate. Continue for about 100 yards alongside a left-hand hedge. At a corner, maintain the direction over the open field to pass through a wooden field gate. In the pasture, continue to a gate on to the A4189. Turn left for 400 yards. Opposite a house on the left, turn right through a gateway (the gate may be missing). The footpath (sign missing) is alongside a right-hand hedge to the motorway fence. Turn left, with the traffic now rushing by on the right.

Climb a far corner stile and stay by the highway, with a new plantation of saplings on the left side. Continue along the well-signed path to a farm cart track by a motorway bridge. Turn left. At a farmstead, pass through gates and continue to a lane. Turn left to the A4189. Turn right, then at once left to a crossroads. Cross to New Road which leads to the New Inn after ⅓ mile.

Wootton Wawen
The Bull's Head

The beautiful old building carries a date, 1387, so it must be one of the oldest pubs in Warwickshire. Whether the place was always a hostelry is doubtful and history does not record it. Perhaps it was a farm or a yeoman's house. The pub is full of character (some say it is haunted), with thick beams supported on uprights 2 ft thick and stone-flagged floors, worn by countless feet over the centuries. There are blazing log fires to welcome visitors in the winter and the dining-room provides old world elegance and is richly furnished.

This is the plaice (sorry!) to come to for the lover of fish dishes. There is every fish dish conceivable chalked on the blackboard, including such delicacies as oysters, lobsters, mussels, crab and squid, besides the usual varieties. The pièce de résistance is the seafood platter, with at least six types to savour. To complement the food (which includes plenty of choice for the non-fish eater as well) we find a separate board listing the wines offered and there is a wide selection of real ales, such as Marston's Pedigree, London Pride from Fuller's, and Morland Old Speckled Hen, plus several guest beers. Children do not have a separate menu but can be catered for. Dogs must remain outside, I'm afraid. The pub is open from 12 noon to 3 pm daily at lunchtimes. Evening hours are from 6 pm to 11 pm (Monday to Saturday) and on Sunday from 7 pm to 10.30 pm.

Telephone: 0564 7925511.

How to get there: The pub is on the A3400 between Birmingham and Stratford-upon-Avon, at the junction with the B4089, in the centre of Wootton Wawen.

Parking: There is a car park at the side of the pub.

Length of the walk: 5 miles. Map: OS Landranger series 151 Stratford-upon-Avon and surrounding area (GR 152632).

The walk mainly follows the banks of two waterways. The start is beside the meandering river Alne (where you may be lucky to spot the elusive kingfisher) and the return leg is along the towing path of the Stratford Canal, completed in 1816 to carry coal southwards and limestone and grain in the opposite direction.

The Walk

From the car park, cross the B4089 to the cul-de-sac estate road called 'The Dale'. At the end go right, by garages, then at once left to walk beside a left-hand wall (with a terrace of houses on the right). Climb a rough railing stile into a pasture. Take the direction arrowed to walk beside hedges to the river Alne. Turn right to climb a step stile between the river and a wire fence. Walk beside the right-hand fence (which surrounds a waterworks). Follow the fence to a stile into a pasture. Make for the far right corner to join a vehicle drive through a gate to a lane.

Turn left to cross the river and immediately turn right to go under the railway to a gate into a pasture. Follow the signed heading and pass through a gateway (no gate). Bear left. The path is now never far from the right-hand river which we 'nudge' near a farmstead on the opposite bank.

In trees, climb a fence stile and continue to a pasture. Bearing slightly left away from the river, make for a railed footbridge now seen. Over a brook, walk the length of a meadow, aiming to the far right corner. Go through a gate to a farm cart track. Follow this to a lane and turn left. Keep on the lane for a little over a mile, then turn left at a signed path to climb a step stile into a field. Cross to the opposite stile. We now cross the long-discarded rail route. This was affectionately known as the 'Coffeepot Line' because (so I am told) of the shape of the locomotive funnel.

Follow the arrowed path over a working railway and climb the gentle hill on the far side, walking alongside the remnants of a right-hand hedge. Climb a stile by a metal gate to join a hedged cart track, then continue ahead. There is a right-hand hedge for 150 yards. Climb a stile, then regain the old heading (left-hand hedge now) to a stile on to a vehicle drive. Turn right.

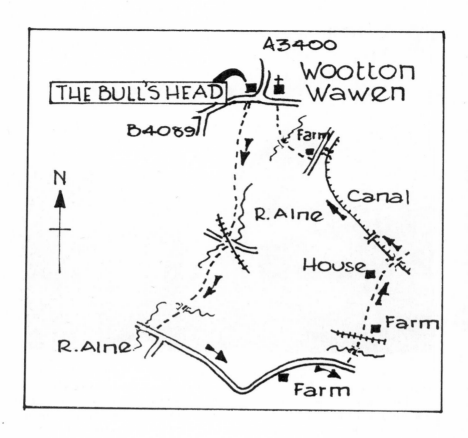

Over the canal bridge, gain the towing path to the left and walk along it, with the water on the left. At the next bridge go over the water. Note the split bridge so the towing ropes of the barges did not have to be unhitched. Continue, with the water now on your right side.

Leave the waterway at the following bridge. Turn left along a vehicle drive (with bungalows on the right) to a lane. Turn left for 100 yards. Go through a kissing-gate on the right. In the pasture, walk by a right-hand fence. Waymarks show the route to the bridge to cross the river Alne. Turn right along a footpath which runs along the top of an old earthwork. Ahead is the tower of Wootton Wawen's church. Keep ahead to the A3400. Turn left and the Bull's Head is reached within about 200 yards.

15 Ufton
The White Hart

Travel along the White Hart Lane and you will not find football played by the Spurs but pétanque by the Wanderers. At the 400-year-old coaching inn there is a large area where this fast-growing pub game (imported from our French friends, of course) can be enjoyed. This is a fun pub where a visit is an occasion, from the friendly welcome from Clive and Karen on arrival, to the final drink. The building was originally a workhouse, accommodating the stonemasons constructing St Michael's church across the lane. Now the bars are stone and oak, with the walls decorated with agricultural implements of days past, and there is a homely, relaxing feeling. But you may be tempted to sit in the garden (where there are plenty of tables and benches), for the view over the chequered countryside of the vale of the river Avon is magnificent. The pub is full of interest. Besides pétanque, you will find traditional darts, football, and dominoes, and stories abound of the pub ghost (a lady). You may also be told of the headless horseman and the phantom coach and horses riding up the hill from the valley.

The range of food and drink in this Greenalls inn is extensive, but it is the 'specials' blackboards (which fill a wall) which take the eye. The choice can be from around 70 main dishes (including over a

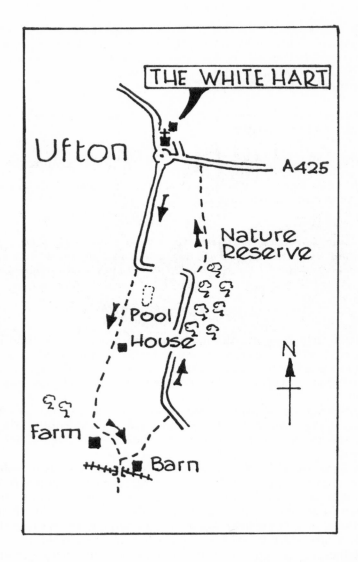

THE WHITE HART

Ufton

A425

Nature Reserve

Pool House

Farm

Barn

N

dozen vegetarian). Many are unusual – how about Hart Porky Rack, barbecue ribs of pork with potato fries, followed by Black Bottom Pie, full of cream and chocolate. Eat after the walk and forget the calorie count for the day. There is a trio of real ales from which to select: Davenports, Tetley or Greenalls Original. There are numerous different coffees too (including the interesting-sounding Parisienne,

Monks and Jamaican). The times of opening are 12 noon to 2.30 pm each day and 7 pm to 11 pm on Monday to Saturday (10.30 pm on Sunday). Fido is asked to stay and admire the view outside, but children are welcome and there is a play area.

Telephone: 0926 612428.

How to get there: The pub is 4 miles south-east of Leamington Spa along the A425, Daventry road.

Parking: There is a large car park behind the pub.

Length of the walk: 3 miles. Map: OS Landranger series 151 Stratford-upon-Avon and surrounding area (GR 379622).

The walk follows the Centenary Way (Warwickshire's long-distance path, completed to mark the 100 years of county administration) through meadowland, with wide vistas westwards. On the return leg there is a nature reserve (administered by the Warwickshire Nature Conservation Trust) through woods and old gravel quarries.

The Walk

From the car park, go to the main road and turn left. At the round-about, cross to the lane signed to Ufton Fields. Within ½ mile, the lane bends sharp left. Here, climb a stile to a meadow on the right. Follow the direction indicated, with a pool where wildfowl play away to the left.

Climb a double step-stile in the opposite boundary and walk by a left-hand hedge. Maintain the direction, passing a white house. Further stiles show the way. Perched on a ridge ahead is the tower of Harbury windmill.

Join a cart track and follow this to a farmstead. The track bears to the left of barns. Just before a railway bridge, leave the Centenary Way by climbing a stile to the left. The path is signed. After two more stiles, bear left to go over a metal railing stile. Continue across the field to an old stile. In the next field walk by a right-hand hedge to a lane. Turn left for a little over ½ mile. Go through a kissing-gate on the right, where the path is signed to Ufton and we enter the nature reserve.

Follow the cinder path alongside a left-hand wire fence. When the path divides, take the left-hand fork to pass through a kissing-gate. Beyond a seat, the path divides again. Take the left-hand fork to immediately climb a stile out of the reserve. Follow the well-walked path to the A425. Turn left. Within 100 yards, take a lane on the right. This is White Hart Lane and will take you to the White Hart pub.

16 Napton-on-the-Hill
The Napton Bridge Inn

The bridge is where the main road crosses over the Oxford Canal. This was undoubtedly a canal age waterway pub where the horses towing the barges were changed and the bargees found refreshment. The stables can still be seen at the rear of the pub, which dates back to Victorian times, around the middle of the last century. It is now a Greenalls tenancy in the hands of John and Lydia, who have, over nearly 20 years, built up a good trade from travellers who have arrived by water, as well as those who have come by land.

In the three bars (cosy, low ceilings, open fires in winter) and restaurant, there is a choice of real ales, Tetley, Davenports and Thomas Greenall's Original. There are also three ciders – Strongbow, Woodpecker and Scrumpy Jack. The wide menu includes Italian cuisine as well as children's and vegetarian sections and one can always find a low price item on the daily specials board. I found the very porky sausages and chips to be wonderful value. Lydia is Italian, so naturally there is also Italian cuisine. The house dog loves to see fellow canine visitors – as long as they are on a lead in the large garden. There is also a children's play area here. The opening hours are flexible.

Telephone: 0926 812466.

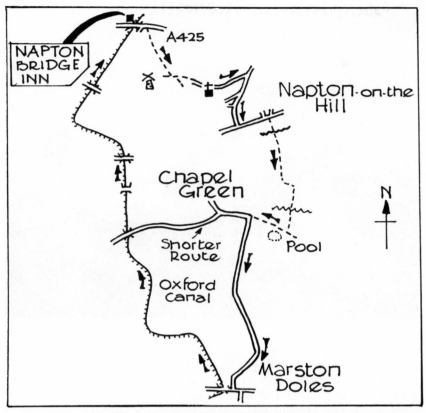

How to get there: The pub is on the main A425 Daventry – Leamington road, 3 miles to the east of Southam.

Parking: There is a large car park at the side of the pub.

Length of the walk: 4 miles or 7 miles. Map: OS Landranger series 151 Stratford-upon-Avon and surrounding area (GR 456620).

The walk climbs the 500 ft high Napton Hill (Napton means village on the hilltop) where there are two towers. The tower of the church of St Lawrence dates from the 18th century and a field or so away is the beautifully restored windmill which records take back to 1543. Whether we choose the longer or the shorter route for the return, we walk along the towing path of the Oxford Canal. The waterway was constructed in the 18th century and the barges had a long tortuous route, the canal being built as a contour canal rather than a 'cut' one.

The Walk

From the car park, turn left on the main road to cross the bridge. Within 200 yards, go over a stile by a road to an industrial estate. The path is signed and points a way up the ridge and furrow pasture to a corner stile on to a rough meadow. Maintain the heading to another stile. Over this, bear 45° left to a stile in the opposite boundary.

In a sheep pasture, walk parallel to the right-hand wire fence to a stile on to a lane. We turn left (but you may like to go right in order to have closer look at the lovely windmill). The lane divides – keep left along a cart track to pass Church Leyes Farm. The notice states it is 'in harmony with nature' and for a modest entrance fee one can tour the farm.

Follow the cart track to pass the church and then go along a lane to descend the hill to the village. Turn right along the main street to pass the village green. At a T-junction, turn left along Dog Lane. At the end of houses on the right, take an unsigned bridleway along a cart track. Go over a brook, then pass through a gate. The route is now beside hedges. Pass through another gate and turn left (left-hand hedge now). At once, in the next pasture, go right to pass a pond. Through a metal hunting gate, walk at the side of a field to go through a metal gate. Turn right.

In a large flat sheep pasture, follow the side of the right-hand wire fence to pass a pool where cup and saucer lilies thrive, to a gate on to a lane. Here you can choose either to return to the pub by way of Chapel Green, or to continue on to Marston Doles, to enjoy a longer stretch of canalside walking on the return journey.

For the shorter walk, turn right on the lane then left at Chapel Green, to the canal. Cross the water and follow the towing path to the right, all the way back to the pub at Napton Bridge.

For the longer walk, turn left to reach the canal at Marston Doles. Gain the towing path and continue with the water on your right-hand side, walking beside the canal to return to the pub.

17 **Harbury**
The Shakespeare

The building is around 500 years old – it was, in those long ago days, three cottages, which were later to become shops to satisfy the needs of a growing town. The Shakespeare has been an inn for just over a century. The ambience is cosy, with a lot of old woodwork and nooks where the world's problems can be forgotten. There are pictures of old country scenes, including Constable's *Haywain* (not the original, of course). Log fires blaze in the wintertime and the garden room is a pleasant dining area. This is a typical rural pub with plenty of activities for the locals. There are darts and pool, football and tug o' war teams. At the summer fête the pub enters a decorated float.

Andrew and Karen Cleaver have been in this Whitbread house for about ten years. In that time they have built up a good reputation for the friendly atmosphere and the culinary delights – all home-made – including the magnificent steak and kidney pie. The children's menu has all the favourites and they especially love the chicken drumsticks, followed by the fruity Shakespeare cocktail. The choice of real ales is between Flowers IPA, Boddingtons, Marston's Pedigree and Wadworth 6X. There are pleasant gardens at the back, with an aviary and rabbits to amuse children. Dogs are allowed if well behaved. The

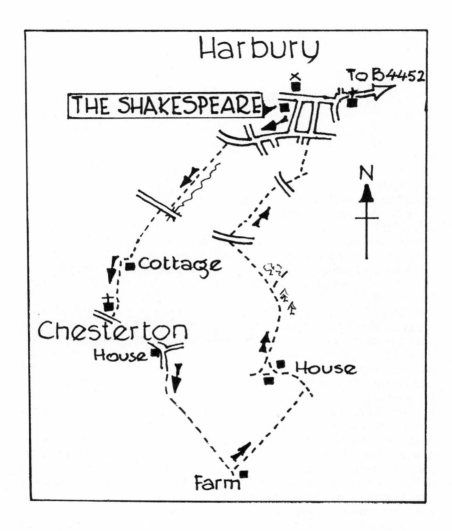

opening hours are 12 noon to 3 pm (Sunday to Friday) and 12 noon to 4 pm on Saturday, with evening hours of 5.30 pm to 11 pm (7 pm to 10.30 pm on Sunday).
  Telephone: 0926 612357.

How to get there: Harbury is 7 miles south-east of Leamington Spa and can be reached from the A425 along the B4452. The Shakespeare is in Mill Street in the centre of the town.

Parking: There is a car park behind the pub.

Length of the walk: 5½ miles. Map: OS Landranger series 151 Stratford-upon-Avon and surrounding area (GR 372600).

The route is through the country town, then over meadows and arable fields. We pass the site of the long-demolished mansion of the Peytos to their large church at Chesterton. Here there are the magnificent tombs of the family and a fine gateway to a design by Inigo Jones. The walk continues along estate roads through wide open fields.

The Walk
From the car park, turn right in Mill Street then at once right again along Chapel Street. At the T-junction continue right, along Park Lane. Follow the road almost out of the town to climb a stile on the left.

Walk through several fields, with stiles showing the way, with a hidden willow-fringed brook on the left. Go over a bridge and stile on to a road. Go right a step or so, then take a signed bridleway on the left. The path hugs the left-hand hedge then goes around the corner to a cottage.

Follow the path around the cottage to a field. It was to the left that the great Peyto house was situated until its destruction in 1902. Now only a garden wall remains to mark the spot. Bearing left, drop down the field to a bridge over the brook. Aiming to the left of the church and Peyto gateway (restored in 1990), go through a lych gate to the churchyard. Follow the arrowed way to a lane. Turn left, with pools for wildfowl on the right side.

Walk along the estate road over a cattle grid. At a junction by a house, take the right-hand fork to a farm. Go to the left, still along farm roads. At a Y-junction, walk left and stay on the 'road' to pass woods. A step or two further (by a private drive), go through a white metal gate to a field on the left. At once, turn right to follow the edge of fields to a road. Turn right for 150 yards. Look for a signed path over a stile on the left. The path goes direct to a road. A step or two to the right, take another path across an arable field.

A few yards past a solitary oak, turn left over a stile. Walk the length of a sports field to a road. Cross to Ivy Lane opposite. This leads to the Bull Ring and a junction. Turn left along High Street to the Shakespeare.

18 Aston Cantlow
The King's Head

This pub is part of our literary history, for it is said that here the parents of William Shakespeare held their wedding breakfast after the ceremony in the nearby church of St John the Baptist. The interior is full of old beams, oaken furniture and settles and gleaming brass. We find a huge inglenook and hidden corners, and, with stone-flagged floors, walkers feel welcomed. Di and Joe Saunders have retained the old-fashioned atmosphere to good effect in this Whitbread house. Outside there is a massive spreading chestnut tree (which offers youngsters prize-sized conkers in autumn) and the 14th century building is swathed in hanging Virginia creeper.

The food menu offers good-value, traditional pub fare. There are always items for vegetarians, and children can find the 'with chips' things that they love. There is a separate children's room, but they may prefer the garden where there are plenty of benches and tables. There is no firm rule on well-behaved dogs – ask the landlord is the answer. The real ales sold are Boddingtons Bitter, Wadworth 6X, Marston's Pedigree and Morland Old Speckled Hen. There is cider (Dry Blackthorn) on draught. The opening hours are 11.30 am to 2.30 pm and 7 pm to 11 pm (Monday to Saturday) and 12 noon to 2.30 pm and 7 pm to 10.30 pm on Sunday.

Telephone: 0789 488242.

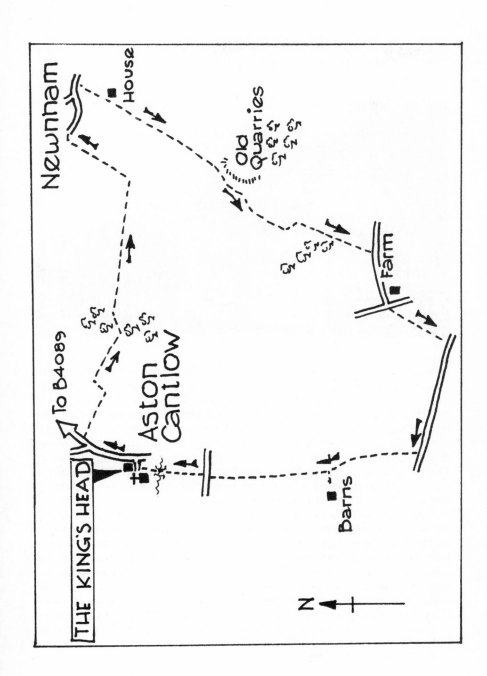

THE KING'S HEAD

To B4089

Newnham

House

Old Quarries

Aston Canlow

Farm

Barns

N

How to get there: Aston Cantlow is signposted from the B4089 Wootton Wawen to Alcester road, south of Henley-in-Arden. The pub is in the centre of the village.

Parking: There is a car park behind the pub.

Length of the walk: 5½ miles. Map: OS Landranger series 151 Stratford-upon-Avon and surrounding area (GR 139599).

You start by walking through the pretty village, which was once important enough to have a Norman castle and a regular market. The route then climbs above the vale, up the wooded ridge called Rough Hills. Over arable lands, we reach the hamlet of Newnham. The return is along bridleways and footpaths, with the tower of Aston Cantlow church acting as a guiding beacon.

The Walk

From the car park, turn left a yard or two along Church Lane to the main street. Turn left, with the pub now on the left. Walk to the far end of the village. When the houses end on the right, there is a footpath signed through a metal gate. Walk directly away from the road. The wide track goes through a gateway (no gate). Turn left along the left-hand hedge, then go 90° to the right in a corner. Continue alongside a left-hand hedge. Through a corner gateway (again no gate), follow the cart track through bushes to the top of the ridge, from where there is an excellent view.

Proceed by a left-hand hedge and keep a constant heading along a clear track. The route goes over open arable fields. On the far side, the way of tractors turns sharp left. Follow the farm track around bends to Newnham and keep ahead past the little green. Within a few steps, turn right, down a farm drive.

Continue past a house and along a bridleway. The direction is fairly constant around the edge of fields. Soon there is a hidden quarry on the left and a reassuring waymark arrow. Climb a step stile by woods to descend over arable lands to a lane.

Turn right. At a junction cross to the opposite gateway. Two paths are signed. Take the left-hand direction, to walk alongside a right-hand hedge to a hedge gap into a lane. Turn right. Within ½ mile, take a signed path over a rather hidden stile on the right. Walk beside a left-hand hedge to join a cart track.

Keep ahead to a lane. Turn right for a couple of steps, then go over a stile to a meadow. Walk the length of it to a stile and bridge under a large willow tree. Keep ahead along a path through the churchyard. Through the lych gate is Church Lane and the King's Head is a few steps to the right.

60

Priors Hardwick
The Butcher's Arms

The inn is said to be even older than the nearby church – unusual this, because in so many villages the two were of the same age, with the inn being used to house the workmen. The area was a great Royalist stronghold during the Civil War and many cannon balls of the battles have been found. You can even see one that was discovered embedded in the pub wall. No doubt the place was also popular with the drovers, as the Welsh Road runs nearby. The ancient buildings have been extended and enhanced in recent years.

This freehouse is a delight in so many ways. Besides the warm welcome, from Lino Pires and his staff, there is the cosy atmosphere where the old-fashioned pub has been grafted skilfully onto a magnificent restaurant. The fame of the food and wine offered has spread far beyond the confines of the beautiful village, as is evidenced by the pictures of celebrities who are lucky enough to have visited the Butcher's Arms. Keg beers, Bass and Brew XI only, are sold – no real ales are stocked. The menu is extensive. Like all the good things in life the prices are not cheap but here you will get something really special to make the visit and the walk memorable. All the food is prepared on the premises. Note that there are no reductions in prices for

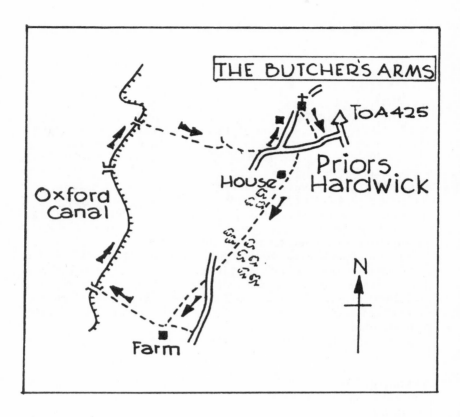

children. The Butcher's Arms is open every day of the year but closed Saturday lunchtime and Sunday evening.

A further delight is the garden, a 4½ acre patch of paradise, with lakes and waterfalls, which is Lino's passionate hobby. 'Some people make money and give nothing back,' said Lino. 'We give them back something extra – our garden.'

Telephone: 0327 60504.

How to get there: Priors Hardwick is 15 miles south-east of Leamington Spa. From the A425 at Napton, turn right along lanes to Priors Hardwick. The pub is in the centre of the village near the church.

Parking: There is a large car park in front of the pub.

Length of the walk: 3½ miles. Map: OS Landranger series 151 Stratford-upon-Avon and surrounding area (GR 470562).

The old church is passed early on this walk. There is much Norman work to admire. There is then a fine upland path along a ridge with extensive views over Warwickshire. The towing path of the 18th century Oxford Canal is used back to Priors Hardwick.

The Walk

From the car park, walk along the lane to the church. Turn right, with the church on the left, to continue through the churchyard to a bridge and kissing-gate into a pasture. Cross to the far corner along a clear path. Go through a kissing-gate to a lane. Turn right. Within 300 yards and by a lay-by, climb a stile to sheep pastures on the left. Bear right to aim just to the left of the distant house. Just 'nudge' the garden, then climb the bank to a far corner fence stile by a wood, into a sown field.

Continue, with the woods on the right, to a corner fence stile. Maintain the heading through sheep pastures to pass a solitary chestnut tree to a wide fence stile into woods. Keep the direction through the trees to a large hill pasture and to a stile onto a lane. The path from the wood may be officially diverted but will be well signed.

Cross to the stile and signed path opposite. Follow the indicated direction over a usually sown field to a farm drive. If the track over the field is difficult, the farmer is happy for walkers to use the drive from the road.

On the farm drive, turn right for 100 yards to pass through metal gates. Follow the cart track through a gateway and onward to a canal bridge. Go over the water. At once turn left over the fence stile to the towing path. Walk northwards, with the water on your right side. After a mile go under a bridge.

Continue along the towing path to the next bridge and leave the canal. Go over the water, then across a sheep pasture to a far gate and climb the fence stile alongside. Keep ahead to join a lane. Still maintain the direction for a few steps. Take the lane left (signed to the village centre). This way leads to the Butcher's Arms.

20 Moreton Morrell
The Black Horse

The Black Horse, once called the Sea Horse, is tucked between houses in the main village street, rubbing eaves with a thatched cottage. It is thus a humble village inn with few pretentions run by Brian Quinney, who knows what locals and travellers (including ramblers) want.

There is a small and cosy bar, the fount of current news both parochial and national, with wooden settles and chairs, and a games room where pool and dominoes are played at the rear. The choice of real ales in this freehouse is between Hook Norton Bitter and a guest beer, which is regularly changed, although the Shepherd Neame from far away Faversham is a popular choice. There are three ciders – Strongbow (on draught), TNT and Diamond White. Tea and coffee is also available (in mugs of course). Girls who are students at the nearby agricultural college often help behind the bar to add a touch of glamour to the pub. The landlord is of the opinion that pubs are pubs rather than restaurants, but I must say that the simple fare offered is ideal for ramblers. The filled baps are the finest I have found on my walks and hot pies sound ideal after a wintertime ramble. The pub, because space is so limited, is not suitable for children and dogs cannot be admitted (no doubt the house lurcher cross would also

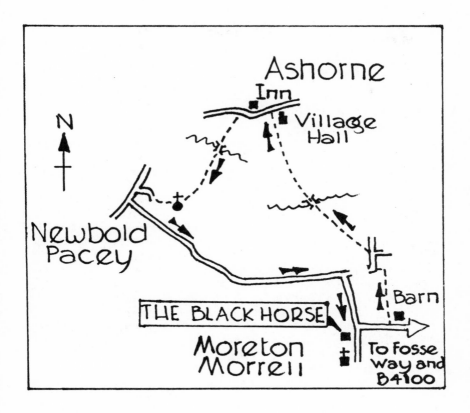

object). The opening hours are 11.30 am to 2.30 pm and 7 pm to 11 pm (Monday to Saturday) and usual Sunday times.
Telephone: 0926 651231.

How to get there: Moreton Morrell is along a lane, 1 mile off the Fosse Way and 7 miles south of Warwick. The pub is in the centre of the village.

Parking: The pub has no car park but you can leave your car in the quiet street outside.

Length of the walk: 4 miles. Map: OS Landranger series 151 Stratford-upon-Avon and surrounding area (GR 311559).

The walk is over some gently attractive countryside. This is intensively farmed land — mixed and arable. The walk goes by a most delightfully sited cricket ground, bordered by a brook at Ashorne, where you may be tempted to linger awhile. On the return route we pass Newbold Pacey church, which was designed by J.L. Pearson, the architect of Truro cathedral.

The Walk

Walk northwards along the main street and turn right, along Brook Lane. Within 200 yards, take a signed path on the left. In the pasture, walk alongside the left-hand border, with a barn on the right, to a far corner stile. Follow the well-waymarked route to a lane. Turn right. Within a few steps, by a junction, a path is signed over a stile on the left.

Take the arrowed direction. The path is through sheep pastures, then crosses a brook over a footbridge. Beyond, walk through fields, taking the yellow arrowed headings. The path leads to a gate by the village hall at Ashorne. Turn left to walk along the main street of the hamlet, passing an inn. About 100 yards beyond and at the end of the hamlet, a path starts on the left. It is signed through a little metal gate, then crosses the picturesque cricket field. Aim to the left of the pavilion.

Cross the brook. The well-used track keeps at the border of a field. Ignore a stile on the right and continue at the side of the field. The path leads to the church at Newbold Pacey. Keep the church on the left and proceed to the drive. Walk along the drive, passing cottages and a little green on the way to the B4087.

Turn left, then immediately left again along a lane signed to Moreton Morrell. Glance right and you may catch a glimpse of Moreton Hall. It was built in 1906 for an American (Mr Garland), who included one of the rare real tennis courts. The building now houses a large agricultural college. At the junction, turn right to the village and the pub.

21 **Wixford**
The Three Horseshoes

The name suggests the blacksmith's craft and – sure enough – we find the old forge (with the ancient tools of the trade) incorporated into this very attractive, restored building, which was once part of the Throckmorton Estate. They still talk of Jack Robbins hereabouts. He was the blacksmith for a long time and his wife Molly ran the adjoining pub for over 50 years, until 1983. This is an inn which preserves the best of the old with the best of the new and also gives a positive and unstinted welcome to walkers. Mike and Jan Shaw in this Whitbread house do not mind a bit of footpath mud on the stone-flagged floors and even have a special stile to lead walkers towards the hostelry. A free leaflet is available which not only extols the merits of the pub but also gives the directions for further walks in this beautiful area of quiet lanes and upland pathways. And how about buying your own steak from the bar and cooking it yourself, just how you like it, on the garden barbecue?

The menu is interesting and enterprising but the favourite items are still the home-made pies, the choice of steak and kidney, chicken and vegetable, and ham and mushroom, all delicious, making the selection difficult. There are plenty of goodies, too, for the vegetarian taste,

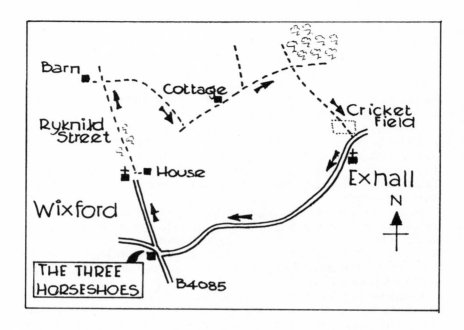

and a children's menu. The youngsters' meals can be taken in the family room or in the family garden. The beers available in this Whitbread house are Flowers Original and IPA and Boddingtons. Dogs must stay outside to admire the garden (sorry Fido and Nell), but it is truly delightful, with a tumbling stream flowing through the grounds.

Telephone: 0789 490400.

How to get there: Wixford is 2 miles north of Bidford on Avon and is on the B4085, which runs between the A439 and the A435. The pub lies on the south side of the village.

Parking: There is a car park at the front and side of the pub.

Length of the walk: 3½ miles. Map: OS Landranger series 150 Worcester and the Malverns (GR 092545).

A narrow lane leads to a church (sadly often locked) where there are unique treasures – huge canopied brasses of Thomas de Crewe and his wife. The walk continues along the track which was the Romans' Ryknild Street, then over hills to little Exhall village.

The Walk

Leave the car park at the exit furthest from the pub. Cross to the lane signed as a 'no through road'. At the end is Wixford's humble church. Keep ahead along the banked track which is Ryknild Street. After a little over ½ mile (where there is a small brick barn on the left), a signed junction of ways is reached. In the field to the left is the mound on which the Norman Ralph de Botoler's castle was perched.

Turn right, along a cart track which is signed as a footpath. At a junction of wide tracks, turn left. We have now gained some height so there is a good view over the valley, with the 17th century Ragley Hall prominent. Pass a cottage on the left. Shortly after, the main farm 'road' bends sharp left. Maintain the former direction ahead along a signed footpath.

Immediately before a wood, turn right. The footpath, which may be unsigned, goes at the side of an arable field alongside a left-hand hedge. Over the ridge is a splendid view across the Avon vale to the Cotswolds. In a corner climb a stile, then turn right a step or two to go over another. Regain the old direction to drop down the hill to a stile to a cricket field.

Continue to a short vehicle track to a lane at Exhall, once named 'Dodging Exhall' because of its inaccessibility. Turn right to pass the 12th century church. Follow the twisting lane to a junction. Bear right to the B4085 and the Three Horseshoes.

22 Avon Dassett
The Prince Rupert Inn

The name gives a clue that we are near Civil War battle territory. Edge Hill is only a mile or so distant and the forces of Prince Rupert would no doubt have passed this way. Not that they would have found refreshment here, for (as pubs go) this is a newcomer. Formerly known as the Avon, it has now been restored and refurbished by Peter Ogden-Jones and his wife Deana, and, as a freehouse, is providing good food and drink in a very pleasant environment – which is splendid for walkers as the long distance Warwickshire footpath of the Centenary Way passes the door.

The décor in the bar, lounge and restaurant is mock-medieval but there is a cosy feel to the place. I especially like the encouragement to families, with a 'Young Cavalier' menu (everything around £1 and served 'with smiling face potatoes') and a fascinating mini farm (piglets, rabbits, ducks, hens and that kind of thing). The beers on offer are Tetley Bitter, Holt's Entire, Aylesbury Best and keg Ansells. The cider is a choice between Autumn Gold and Dry Blackthorn. The menu concentrates on simple, sustaining food, with a 'chef's special' and plenty of salads always available. The hours of opening are 12 noon to 2.30 pm and 7 pm to 11 pm (Monday to Saturday, possibly extended in the summer months). Normal Sunday times.

Telephone: 0295 89270.

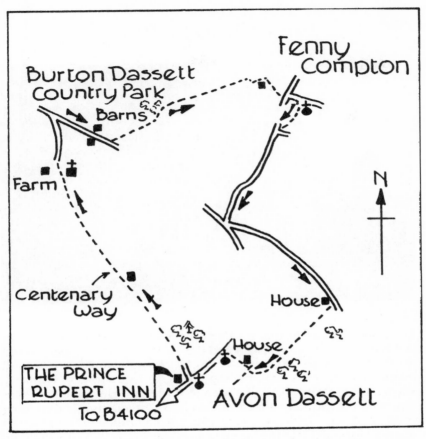

How to get there: The village of Avon Dassett is 8 miles north of Banbury off the B4100. The pub is in the village centre.

Parking: There is a car park at the rear of the pub.

Length of the walk: 5 miles. Map: OS Landranger series 151 Stratford-upon-Avon and surrounding area (GR 410500).

After fairly level farmland, the route climbs steeply to the uplands of the Burton Dassett Country Park. This is an area where limestone has been quarried spasmodically over the centuries but where sheep now graze. The return leg is from Fenny Compton – a village of honey-hued stone and a church where soldiers took refuge after the Battle of Edge Hill.

The Walk

Out of the car park, turn left in front of the pub, then at once left down a cul-de-sac. At the end, pass through two metal gates to parkland. The route from here to the Burton Dassett Hills is the Centenary Way and is well waymarked with bold arrows. Bear slightly right across the parkland to pick up the side of a hedge. This is on your right for some distance to a bridge across a brook.

Cross the open arable field, beyond, to a distant stile into sheep pastures. There is now a series of arrowed stiles to the lovely Norman church, which is called the Cathedral on the Hills. Keep ahead along the vehicle way (passing an ancient well) and lane to climb to a junction. Turn right to go over the cattle grid out of the country park.

Pass barns on each side of the road. About 400 yards beyond, go through a double metal railing gate on the left. In a hill pasture walk by a right-hand wire fence, going downhill towards a wood. Go through a gate by a sheep pen and follow the arrowed direction, now with the woods on the left.

Proceed to the very far end of a rough pasture. Pass through a metal gate (another arrow) then walk at the side of an arable field, alongside a left-hand hedge. Around a far corner to the right, go through a gate and cross a pasture to a gate by a barn. Turn right in front of the barn to climb a step stile. Follow the path to a road at Fenny Compton.

Turn left, then right down Church Street. Within 200 yards, go right (Dog Lane) to pass the church. Keep ahead to pass Hall Yard Cottage and go through a barrier. Follow this way to a road. Turn right then, by the fine signpost depicting the Warwickshire emblem (a bear and ragged staff), turn left to climb the hill.

At a crossroads, turn left. Within ½ mile and just past a house, climb a log stile on the right. In a sheep meadow, walk directly away from the road to pass above old quarry workings (on the right). Continue ahead to climb a far stile. Walk along a path, alongside a left-hand wire fence. Go through a gate and climb out of the valley by a right-hand fence.

Climb a stile to a vehicle way. Turn right through a metal gate, then at once turn left through a barrier. Proceed to another barrier then follow the path through a wood and churchyard to a lane. Turn left. The Prince Rupert is reached after 300 yards, on the right.

23 Edge Hill
The Castle Inn

This is an inn steeped in history – mine hosts John and Gill Blann make the most of it and why not? The battle of Edge Hill was the opening skirmish of the Civil War in 1642 and it is on the site of the Castle Inn that Charles raised the Royalist standard before his troops descended into the vale where the Parliamentarians were assembled under Lord Essex. The inn itself is a sham castle, built by Sanderson Miller a hundred years after the battle, and modelled on Guy's Tower at Warwick Castle. One bar is a reminder of the war, with maps of the battle stratagem, a fine mural of the fighting and numerous pistols, swords and breastplates of the period. The second bar depicts more peaceful and rustic pursuits, with the walls adorned with agricultural implements. There is one interesting later feature – a print of an aircraft. The Pioneer was one of the first experimental jet aircraft and it was at Edge Hill airfield (long closed by the Royal Air Force) that much of the test flying was undertaken in 1942.

The stone pub, first licensed in 1822, may have a rugged, weather-worn exterior but inside there has been an extensive refurbishing operation by the Hook Norton Brewery. There is a warm cosy look about the beamed bars, the carpets are a homely red and an open fire blazes in the wintertime. John and Gill take great pride in their food.

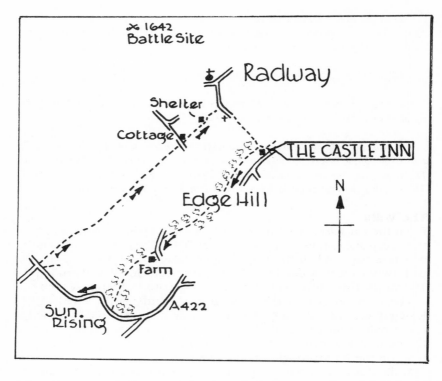

The menu concentrates on simple, wholesome meals and folk travel many miles along the lanes to sample the home-cooked gammon and pies. The mixed grill is also recommended, the 'mix' being of such generous proportions that the plates are extra large – sounds tempting doesn't it after walking the last mile up the steep hill? Children are especially catered for and they invariably plump for the beans on toast with sausage. There is always a vegetarian dish available. The beers on offer are the real ale Hook Norton Bitter and there is also always a guest beer from the Independent Family Brewers of Britain. In addition there are 16 country wines, such as dandelion and cowslip and, for something stronger, an extensive range of malt whiskies. Opening hours are flexible but are based on 11.30 am to 2.30 pm and 6.30 pm to 11 pm.

Choose the right day for your walk and sit in the lovely hilltop garden for your refreshment, where the views are truly magnificent – and your cares will be forgotten. My well-behaved collie Nell was made most welcome and concurs with my observations.

Telephone: 0295 670255.

How to get there: Edge Hill lies between the A422 Banbury – Stratford road and the B4086. It is signposted from Sun Rising Hill, the steep ridge 6 miles north-west of Banbury.

Parking: The car park is opposite the pub.

Length of the walk: 4 miles. Map: OS Landranger series 151 Stratford-upon-Avon and surrounding area (GR 373474).

The walk starts along the high wooded ridge with many clearances for lovely views across the valley, where the great battle took place on Sunday 23rd October 1642. The actual site, however, is on Ministry of Defence land and not open to the public. The return is across farmland where the paths are not so clearly defined.

The Walk

From the car park, cross the road to a signed path. Within a step or two, keep ahead now on the Centenary Way. The path is along a railed concrete path. When the way divides, take the left-hand track. The path twists a well-walked way to a tarmac vehicle track. Turn left for 100 yards, then turn right along a signed path bordering a farm.

The path keeps near the edge of woodlands to the A422 at Sun Rising (there was once an inn of this name here). Drop down the hill for ⅓ mile. Take care as this is a busy road. There is a signed path on the right. A few yards further, take another path (directly opposite a road on the left) through a wide hedge gap.

Walk alongside a right-hand hedge. When this ends, maintain the heading over an open field. Aim to the right of a distant spire. Go over a ditch and through a hedge gap on the far side. Bear right to the far right-hand corner of a field. Under a willow tree, climb a fence stile. Continue ahead for a few yards to go through an old metal railing gate. Walk alongside a left-hand hedge to gates to a lane.

Cross directly over through a gate to the right of a cottage. Keep ahead through a kissing-gate to sheep pastures. Maintain the heading to pass to the right of a brick animal shelter. Climb a corner stile, then keep ahead to another.

The path is now bordered by gravestones. This was the site of the old Radway church, where the bells are said to have rung when the King's troops passed by. A new church was built on another site in 1866.

On a lane by a duck pond, turn right. At the end of the lane, go through a kissing-gate. Now aiming for the pub tower, climb through pastures to a stile by woods. Join the outward path to return to the car park.

24 Middle Tysoe
The Peacock Inn

This is the typical village inn – a real centre of the community and a focus for gatherings and for publicising rural events. There are music nights, a wide selection of traditional pub games, quiz, darts and dominoes teams. Outside, the old Midlands game of Aunt Sally is played with great enthusiasm and success in the competitive league. Alan Cox, who runs this Whitbread house with his wife Kate, is unsure of the precise age of the building but local people say that one end was used as a mortuary for those killed at Edge Hill in the great battle of 1642. The place was obviously extended over the centuries to create the very long building it now is. There is a cosy bar where the open fire is a welcome sight on winter days. Further along is the red-carpeted lounge with its warm ambience, then the small restaurant.

The fare can be chosen from three listings. There are two menus – one for the main meals and another for snacks – and specials for the day are chalked on a board above the lounge fireplace. The choice (many are vegetarian dishes) is impressive and the selection of fish dishes, including Nile perch (from Lake Victoria), calamares, and trout fillet, is particularly good. Local game (especially pheasant, rabbit, pigeon and venison) is very popular in season. The beers to accompany these magnificent dishes are Theakston Best Bitter and XB and also Flowers Original. Heineken and Stella Artois lagers, and cider

are also available. The pub welcomes parties of ramblers (for coffee breaks, as well as lunches). Children will feel quite comfortable here, too – there is a large garden with patio tables and benches. The house dogs, Toby and Beau, are happy to welcome well-behaved canine visitors during the flexible opening hours.
Telephone: 0295 680338.

How to get there: The A422 is the main road between Banbury and Stratford-upon-Avon. About mid-distant and below Edge Hill, turn along the lane signed to Tysoe. Within 2 miles Middle Tysoe is reached. The Peacock is on the right soon after entering the village.

Parking: The car park is behind the inn.

Length of the walk: 5½ miles. Map: OS Landranger series 151 Stratford-upon-Avon and surrounding area (GR 340442).

There are many Windmill Hills in the land but few that are actually topped by a mill – we climb such a hill, however, early on this walk. The hill overlooks the great house of Compton Wynyates. The mansion (unfortunately not open to the public) was built, in brick, in Tudor times and is the seat of the Marquis of Northampton. After a stretch of lane walking, the route back to the village is along part of the Centenary Way, the long-distance path that commemorates the 100 years of local government by Warwickshire County Council.

The Walk
From the car park, turn right to the main village street. Turn right. Keep ahead at junctions to walk along the Shipston Road through Upper Tysoe. At the far end of the village the road twists sharp left then right. Just past a railing bridge go through a field gate on the left.
    In an often arable field, gain the left-hand border to walk alongside a hedge which gradually climbs the hill. Keep by the hedge to pass through a corner gateway (the gate may be missing). Continue climbing to the wonderful windmill.
    Pass just to the left of the mill to climb over a fence stile which is to the left of trees. In a hill pasture walk to a fence stile in the far right-hand corner. Continue the descent, passing an old barn. Go through a corner metal gate. Keep ahead to pass through further gates to a lane. Turn right. Keep ahead at a junction to reach a T-junction and turn right.
    The road passes a farm entrance then, over a bridge, bears right. At once, over the bridge, turn left through a gate and along a signed bridle-way. Keep at the edge of the field, beside a hidden brook (on the left). Pass through a gate into the next field and maintain the direction.

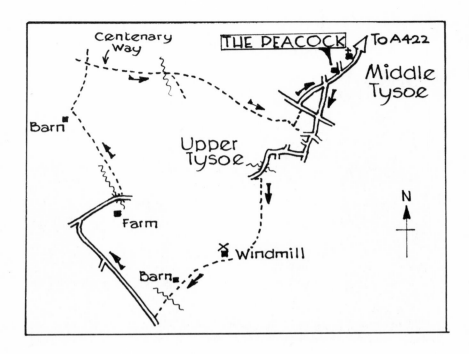

There is a metal gate and bridle gate to the following field, a bridle gate to the third field and another bridle gate to the next, with a waymark arrow here. When level with a barn in the field left, turn 45° right to cut over the open field to a gate in the opposite boundary.

At once go through a bridle gate. Follow the arrowed direction in an often sown field to pick up the Centenary Way path, which crosses our bridleway. Turn right along the Way to climb a stile. Now in a large sheep pasture, follow the arrowed direction to a distant stile. Walk by the left-hand border of an often arable field to pass through a corner gap. Over a stile cross a brook, using the stepping stones.

Here we leave the Centenary Way, which is arrowed. We go slightly left of the Way to a new step-stile. In the next field walk to the far left-hand corner. Continue by the left-hand border to go through a hedge gap. Maintain the heading (never far from the left-hand borders) to a rather hidden step stile into a ridge and furrow pasture. Bear 45° left to a metal railing gate to the left of bungalows.

Cross a small pasture to a new step-stile. Follow the fenced way at the borders of gardens to a 'maze' of wooden barriers. Turn left along a hard path (hedge on the right) to a lane. Cross to Sandpits Road, which leads to Main Street. The Peacock Inn is to the left.

25 Ilmington
The Red Lion

I have included the two pubs in Ilmington because nearby is the best countryside for rambling in Warwickshire and also because they are so different. The Red Lion was for most of its 200-year history a basic country inn, supplying the simple but wholesome wants of agricultural workers. Indeed the Court Baron met here to discuss who would farm where, prior to the Enclosure Acts. Although very few villagers are now employed on the six farms in the vicinity, this Hook Norton Brewery pub still has a rustic appearance, with small bars, stone flags on the floor and so on. The old blacksmith's shop next door is now the inn's garage. There are prints of village scenes of days long past and on the bar wall is a feature on the traditional Ilmington morris dancers, who are to be seen and heard in the area in the summer months. Do the walk on the right Sunday in April and you will see them dancing in the ten village gardens open for charity.

The Red Lion is lovingly cared for by Bob and Ellie Johnson, with a homely feel, masses of gleaming brass, open fires in winter, flowers from the lovely garden and tumbling blooms in baskets and window boxes in summer, and so on. You can join in traditional pub games here, too. The menu includes the usual pub fare and the gammon and

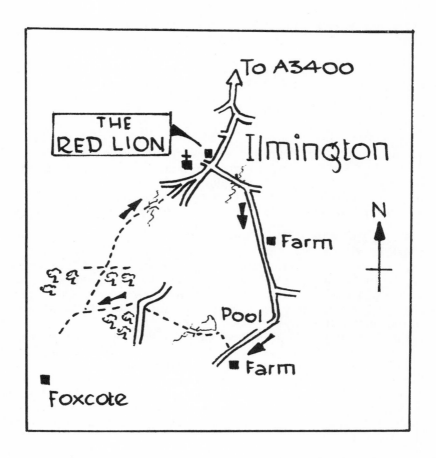

eggs is popular after the hike up the hills – the modest prices are very popular too. The real ales are Old Hooky and Hooky Best Bitter. Well-behaved children (and dogs) are welcome. The hours of opening are 11 am to 2.30 pm and 6.30 pm to 11 pm, with the normal Sunday opening hours.

Telephone: 0608 682366.

How to get there: Ilmington is 8 miles from Stratford. The turning from the A3400 is signposted 4 miles to the south. The Red Lion is on the right in the village.

Parking: Very limited parking is available in front of the pub. Otherwise you can park in the road.

Length of the walk: 3 miles. Map: OS Landranger series 151 Stratford-upon-Avon and surrounding area (GR 212435).

The walk climbs steeply through sheeplands to Ilmington Downs. On the way we pass a pool constructed a few years ago – it is interesting to note how quickly plant and bird-life have become established along the banks. There is also much evidence of badgers in this attractive area.

The Walk

From the Red Lion, take the lane signed to Shipston. We cross a hidden brook, which once supplied the water for sheep dipping, then bear right along a narrow road (signed Compton Scorpion). After 1½ miles and opposite Southfields Farm, a footpath is signed on the right, through a gate. Follow the way of tractors through further gates to a pool.

Swing left (with the pool now on the right) and cross the little rivulet at the far end. The faint path now leads to a corner gate to sheep pastures. Climb the hill, keeping near the left-hand border. At the top of the ridge climb a stile and cross to the drive opposite – this is also signed as a footpath. Within ⅓ mile, take a path to the right. The large mansion in the vale is Foxcote, built in the Palladian style in the early 18th century.

Climb the edge of a usually arable field, keeping by a right-hand border. At the summit cross a wide track. Walk alongside a right-hand hedge. Walk through meadowland, gradually dropping down the hill. Ignore a path going over a stile to the right and continue to a footbridge to cross a brook. Over the water, at once turn left to a corner stile – a bit boggy here. Follow the well-used and waymarked path ahead to meet a lane to Ilmington and a well-deserved drink at the Red Lion.

26 Ilmington
The Howard Arms

Ilmington is perhaps the prettiest village in Warwickshire. It is cupped below the highest hills in the county and splendid walking country – the start of the Cotswolds – and over many centuries butter-hued limestone has been quarried locally to construct the lovely buildings. Overlooking the trim lower green is this renowned freehouse where two of the partners, Melanie Smart and Alan Thompson (who is also the chef), assisted by Lorna the manageress, provide magnificent fare before or after your walk 'over the hills and far away'. The history of the buildings is a little obscure but the oldest section dates from around 1610. The original use was perhaps for farm worker's cottages and coaching stables but there was obviously close association with the Canning and Howard families up at the great house of Foxcote.

Today the pub (where there are also two attractive rooms for bed and breakfast) is a cosy haven where log fires blaze in wintertime. The choice of home-cooked food chalked on the board above the fireplace is truly scrumptious. There are frequent changes of menu and you are tempted with many delicacies. Some are well known, such as steak and kidney pie or salmon, but how about being adventurous with wild boar pâté or game, preceded by nettle soup? Like all the best things

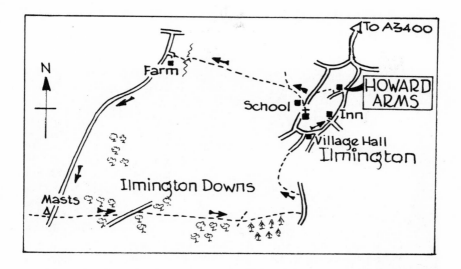

in life, the food does not come at a low price, but here you will savour a meal to remember.

To accompany your meal there is a good selection of beers. The local Flowers Best Bitter is alongside Marston's and Boddingtons. When I called there was also Adnams, all the way from Suffolk. You may well spot well-known faces in the bar – the pub is a favourite with actors from the RSC at Stratford. Outside there is a secluded garden where children can play. Dogs, however, are not particularly encouraged by the house labradors. The opening hours are 11 am to 2.30 pm and 6.30 pm to 11 pm, but are subject to some variation (on Sundays and in winter).

Telephone: 0608 682226.

How to get there: Ilmington is 8 miles from Stratford. The turning from the A3400 is signposted 4 miles to the south. The Howard Arms is in the centre of the village.

Parking: There is a car park to the front and rear of the pub.

Length of the walk: 5 miles. Map: OS Landranger series 151 Stratford-upon-Avon and surrounding area (GR 214437).

The walk climbs to about 9,000 ft along an ancient drovers' road, so the views are really stunning. On the way a pool is passed. This is fed from a chalybeate spring found in 1684, which might well have turned Ilmington village into a spa town.

The Walk

From the Howard Arms, walk a step or two towards the shop and post office. At once there is an unsigned footpath, squeezed between houses on the right. Follow the hard path at the back of gardens to a lane. Turn left. Immediately before the school turn right, through a kissing-gate which was erected to commemorate the Queen's Coronation in 1953.

Follow the fenced way to a stile into a pasture. There is now a well waymarked route with further stiles showing the way through the fields, maintaining the same general direction. Pass to the right of the pool. The path then climbs the slope beside a left-hand hedge. Ignore paths signed over stiles to the left to continue along the waymarked route. Drop down to brooks, then proceed to a farm vehicle way to a lane.

Turn left to climb the hill at Larkstoke. At the summit there are radio masts and a farm vehicle track. Take the path opposite. Walk alongside a left-hand wall at the edge of a field. Pass through a corner gate into the next field. Cross a meadow, passing a huge oak tree to a kissing-gate on to a lane. Turn left, then at once right. The vehicle drive is shown as a bridleway. Follow this to a lane.

Turn left for 300 yards and take a signed path on the left. The path crosses a field to a stile. Keep ahead, then bear right to a gate to a wide track. This becomes Grump Street near cottages and descends past the upper green. At a junction by the village hall, turn right along a road to the Howard Arms and those tempting dishes.

27 Shipston-on-Stour
The Horseshoe Inn

This magnificent coaching inn in the picturesque Cotswold town of Shipston has been welcoming travellers for 300 years. The herring-boned, timber-framed front is always a mass of colour in summertime, with tumbling blooms from window boxes and hanging baskets, and there is a secluded terrace garden at the rear, away from the traffic. A friendly ambience pervades the establishment and you can relax in beamed bars or in the restaurant, where there are interesting prints of the town of yesteryear.

There is a huge board on which the bill of fare is chalked – all at most reasonable prices. The humble steak and kidney pie is particularly impressive, 'Yes I know all pubs have this but try ours – we make this ourselves and by golly it's good,' we are modestly informed! Then there are the double decker sandwiches, 'You will have your hands full with this'. There is a special children's menu, and always a good vegetarian selection. Lovers of beer will find a wide range. There is a choice not only of real ales (Brew XI, Ruddles and John Smith's) but also nine imported brews. If country wines are your tipple, there are ten listed. Ciders are Red Rock and Scrumpy Jack. Bed and breakfast is also available at the Horseshoe. Dogs are welcomed and

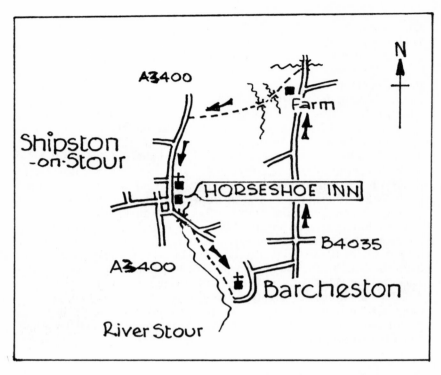

offered a drink – tap water, of course. The pub is open from 11 am
to 3 pm and 7 pm to 11 pm Monday to Friday. Sunday hours are
rather less, but on Saturdays the place is open all day.
Telephone: 0608 663762.

How to get there: The Horseshoe Inn is in the centre of Shipston in
Church Street – a few doors south of the church.

Parking: There is a car park through the arch.

Length of the walk: 3 miles. Map: OS Landranger series 151 Stratford-
upon-Avon and surrounding area (GR 260405).

*The walk starts in the interesting town of Shipston. As the name implies, this was
a place which became prosperous from the sheep and wool industry. The church
tower has looked over the town for 500 years. The walk is along the valley of the
river Stour and we visit another old church – Barcheston has a Pisa-like leaning
tower. The village witnessed the birth of tapestry weaving in England when William
Sheldon set up his looms in the 16th century.*

The Walk

Turn left from the car park to walk away from the church. Bear left along the B4035 to cross the bridge over the river Stour. Note the former flour mill nearby – now the building is a restaurant. Within 200 yards, climb a step stile to a pasture on the right. Take the arrowed direction, keeping by right-hand borders, with the river away to the right. Further stiles show the way through the fields. When in a sheep pasture, with a church tower directly on the left, bear left to the far left corner. Here there is a stile on to a vehicle track.

Within a step or two the track leads to a lane. Follow this left. We go by the church whose tower leans about 1 ft in 50, but we are assured it has not moved for 200 years. At a junction take the right-hand fork. Brailes Hill – one of the highest hills in the county and surmounted by a circular wood – is on the far horizon.

At a T-junction, turn left, then cross the B4035. Stay on the lane for about another mile, passing two junctions. Just before a railed foot-bridge, the next path starts on the left. The stile is a little hidden, back from the lane. In the meadow, continue to the far left corner to cross a footbridge. This is over waters which once powered Fell Mill.

Take the indicated direction to go over the main channel of the river, where fine cup and saucer lilies bloom in summer. In a large pasture, keep by the right-hand border to a vehicle track to the A3400. Turn left to Shipton and the Horseshoe.

28 Lower Brailes
The George Hotel

It is no coincidence that the church opposite the George Hotel is dedicated to St George. In 1350 the masons building the church were housed in the pub building. Ale was dispensed on the site before this, because a market had been granted to Brailes in 1248, and the George claims to be one of the earliest ale houses in Warwickshire. During the age of the Royal Mail coaches, it was a celebrated coaching inn where there was extensive stabling. It may be ancient but it is undoubtedly also one of the nicest rural hotels with the comforts of today. Jane and Peter Brown have run the hotel a relatively short time, but have managed quite a transformation. Six en suite bedrooms are available and in the gleaming stone-flagged restaurant and two bars of this Hook Norton house there is a cosy ambience with huge inglenook fireplaces (one comparatively recently uncovered). The front of the hotel is bedecked with flowers in summertime and the rear gardens, where there are plenty of benches and tables, are a delight and have a winding level path with handicapped folk in mind.

Two Hook Norton real ales are served, together with a brand of guest beers which is changed periodically. The food is all prepared on the premises. The favourites are honey roast duck and a fixed-price

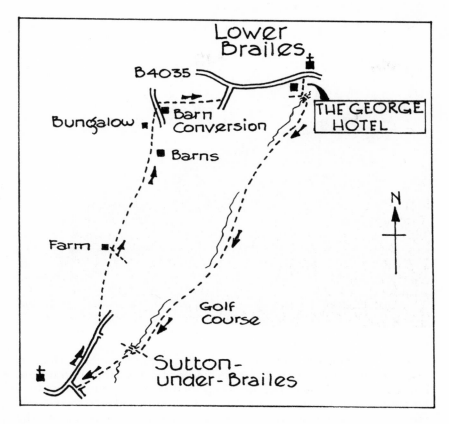

package deal of a soup tureen, cheese board and a bottle of wine. The opening times are normal pub hours. Dogs are welcome on leads. Children are welcome without leads and can have small portions from the menu.

Telephone: 0608 685223.

How to get there: Lower Brailes lies east of Upper Brailes, on the B4035 Shipston to Banbury road. The George Hotel is in the centre of the village, almost opposite the church.

Parking: The car park is at the side of the pub.

Length of the walk: 3½ miles. Map: OS Landranger series 151 Stratford-upon-Avon and surrounding area (GR 313392).

In medieval times Brailes was a thriving and very prosperous wool town – the third largest in the county. The magnificent church is evidence of this wealth and is called the Cathedral of the Feldon (the fertile land in the south of the county). There are two hills overlooking the area – one was topped by a motte and bailey castle and the other is Brailes Hill, which is the second-highest point in the county.

The Walk

Alongside the pub, near the archway through which coaches trundled, take the unsigned footpath. Soon go over a stile and continue to the end of the wall, where there is a junction of pathways. Take the way to the left to cross a brook and climb a stile to a meadow. Turn right at once, with the brook now on your right-hand side. The next field is often sown. Keep ahead to a rather hidden fence stile in the far right-hand corner. Join a farm drive and, as this sweeps left to the farm, maintain the old direction to pass through a metal gate, then at the bottom of a field go over a stile to a golf course. Keep the former direction, with the brook still to the right, to a stile out of the golf course on to a cart track. Turn right, then at once left over a stile into a rough pasture. Bear right to cross the brook over a railing bridge. Gradually leave the brook, with a farmstead away to the right, to reach a rough metal fence, then go over a ditch and a step stile into a pasture.

Follow the arrowed direction to join a cul-de-sac lane by a cottage. Follow the lane a few steps to a T-junction. Turn right to the village of Sutton-under-Brailes. At a T-junction, the 13th century church is to the left but we turn right. Within ¼ mile, the next path is signed through a hedge gap on the left. Take the direction arrowed to cross an open field, aiming for a point to the right of a distant farmhouse. Climb a fence stile under a tree and maintain the direction to cross the farm drive, using two fence stiles.

Go over a little pasture to pass through a gate to a large arable field. Still the direction is constant, passing just to the right of two isolated trees to a distant stile. Cross a sheep pasture to a step stile, then an arable field, making for just to the left of distant barns. Go over a wire fence, plank bridge and step stile into a pasture. Walk across this towards a point to the right of a far bungalow. Go through a bridle gate to a lane.

Turn left for a few steps. At the far side of a barn conversion on the right, climb a stile. Take the signed direction. Stiles show the route (now aiming towards the church tower). Pick up the line of a left-hand hedge, then walk at the side of gardens to a road. Turn left to the B4035. Lower Brailes and the George Hotel are to the right.

29 Cherington
The Cherington Arms

The pub looks very ancient – as indeed the building truly is – but it has only been the hostelry of the pretty little village since the last Great War. Before that it was a general store. The Hook Norton tenancy here is very much a family affair held by Richard Cox with assistance from his wife Wendy (in charge of the kitchen) and son and daughter, and there is a friendly, welcoming atmosphere to the place. The bar has a utilitarian tiled floor to withstand walking boots and there are log fires in the winter months in the inglenook fireplace. The garden backing onto the river Stour is a peaceful haven on warmer days. It is big enough for youngsters to chase and play in and they love to see the colourful birds in the aviary.

The reputation of the meals at the Cherington Arms is widespread. There is a bar menu, with special sections for children, including 'golden tiddlers' and hot-dogs – all with chips of course. The vegetarians have a wide choice on the menu. Were I not to like my meat, I would probably be tempted by the mélange Bourguinonne or brown bean chasseur. The restaurant offers an even larger selection and, like the bar and lounge, the dining-room is cosy and snug. A Sunday roast is also available every week. The opening hours are

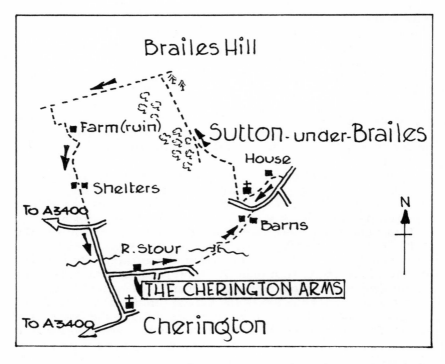

11.30 am to 2.30 pm and 6 pm to 11 pm (Monday to Saturday). Sunday hours are 12 noon to 2 pm and 7 pm to 10.30 pm. Real ales on offer are Hook Norton and Flowers Best Bitter.
Telephone: 0608 75233.

How to get there: Cherington is signed from the A3400 just 1½ miles south of Shipston-on-Stour. A little after 2 miles you will see signs to the Cherington Arms.

Parking: The car park is opposite the pub.

Length of the walk: 3 miles. Map: OS Landranger series 151 Stratford-upon-Avon and surrounding area (GR 292369).

Cherington has nothing to do with cherries — in spite of the pub sign of a buxom lady with an armful of fruit. It means 'a village of the church'. This 13th century building is across a meadow. The walk follows the valley of the Stour to Sutton-under-Brailes, Brailes being the hill which we then climb to give us that thirst at the welcoming Cherington Arms.

The Walk

From the car park, turn right along the lane. Within ¼ mile, the lane bends sharp right. Keep ahead along a footpath beside a left-hand wall to pass a former chapel (now a house). Climb a stile into a pasture.

Bear left to the river Stour. Away to the right are the hollows and banks where there was once a moated house. Follow the river to the right and cross the water over a railed bridge. In the field, make for the double step-stile in the fence to the right of barns. Bear left between the barns to the drive and continue to the green at Sutton-under-Brailes. Maintain the heading along the road to pass the war memorial.

Soon after, by a huge tree stump which serves as the village notice board, turn left along a vehicle drive. Keep to the left of the house at the far end to walk along a fenced footpath to a churchyard. Follow the path past the church with its 14th century tower, to a road.

Turn right, but at once take a signed footpath over a stile to the right. Walk to another stile into a rough pasture, which you cross. Go over a stile to an arable field and follow the arrowed direction to a concreted cart track. Turn right. We soon walk beside a wood, then go through a gate to pastureland. Maintain the direction alongside a wire fence. Nearing the top of the hill, go through another gate.

Continue along the cart track and pass through the corner gate ahead. There is another gate with a blue waymark arrow to the right which you should ignore. At once turn left (left-hand hedge) to go through a corner hunting gate. Maintain the heading over an open sheep pasture where the views are wide and beautiful.

Pass through a hedge gap and immediately turn left, with a left-hand hedge. Go through a corner gate. Turn left to a waymark post. Turn right alongside the field boundary, with a ruined farmhouse on the left-hand side. Within 100 yards, go through a gate on the left, then regain the old heading, now with a right-hand hedge.

Pass through a corner gateway into a field with gorse bushes. Follow the farm track, which soon bears right to a metal gate. Continue downhill by right-hand borders of fields and pass animal shelters to a gate on to a road.

Take the lane opposite. Cross the river Stour to a road junction. The Cherington Arms is ¼ mile to the left.

30 Little Compton
The Red Lion Inn

The village of Little Compton is the most southerly in Warwickshire and the Red Lion Inn is therefore also the southernmost pub. The village is in magnificent upland countryside and is off the main road. Sarah and David Smith, the tenants of this Donnington pub, have had to build up a reputation for good food, ale and hospitality to encourage customers to venture to this quiet rural backwater. That they have succeeded is obvious. Approval by Egon Ronay and Les Relais Routiers are added accolades. The house has been licensed for around 100 years. Prior to this there was a smallholding here, dating back to the 16th century. The cosy beamed lounge has an interesting collection of photos of country scenes of bygone ages and there are many subtly lit corners.

Besides the Donnington real ales, a good selection of lagers and ciders is available. There is a standard menu and 'specials for the day' and vegetarian meals are also served. The Red Lion is renowned for its delicious rump steaks, which are cut to the size required by the customer – the record is a massive 48 oz! Lovers of fish also come to sample the North American redfish fillets cooked in spicy seasoned breadcrumbs. Children are welcomed and can order half portions. It is made clear, however, for health reasons, that dogs do not find a similar welcome. Overnight accommodation is available, including Nookey Hall – the honeymooners' suite. At the rear of the pub is an old world garden and a separate play area for children. The weekday hours are from 11 am to 2.30 pm and 6 pm to 11 pm. On Sundays the pub is open from 12 noon to 2 pm and 7 pm to 10.30 pm.

Telephone: 0608 74397.

How to get there: Little Compton is signed from the A44 Chipping Norton road, 4 miles south-east of Moreton-in-Marsh. The Red Lion Inn is 300 yards on the left just before entering the village.

Parking: The car park is alongside the pub.

Length of the walk: 3 miles or 5 miles. Map: OS Landranger series 151 Stratford-upon-Avon and surrounding area (GR 258302).

The hills in South Warwickshire are nudging the Cotswolds and rise to over 600 ft. There are, therefore, spectacular views over lonely countryside. A few miles distant are historic stone circles and an isolated boulder – the King Stone – around which tales of folklore are woven. In Little Compton is a fine church with a 14th century tower and a manor house which for centuries was the home of the Juxon family.

The Walk
Leave the car park alongside the pub and turn left along the lane signed as a cul-de-sac. Keep to the left of the little post office. Continue ahead, to pass a waymark post and walk along a green pathway. Just

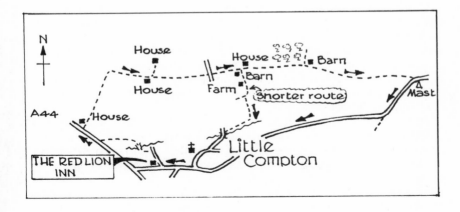

before a bridge over a brook, turn left. The path twists a way through the trees to a wooden footbridge over the brook.

In the field (often arable) turn 45° left. Cross the open field to pass through a hedge gap. Maintain the heading to a stile on to the A44 in the far distant corner. Turn right. Within a few hundred yards, turn right along a wide vehicle way. A house is now on the left-hand side. The track climbs, then turns sharp right.

Just after a house on the right, the vehicle drive sweeps left to a large mansion. We keep ahead along a bridleway and follow this to a lane. Cross to the bridleway opposite and reach a barn. You can return to Little Compton by a shortened route from here, if you wish.

For the shorter walk, turn right just past the barn to walk along a cart track with a hedge on the left side. Just before a farmhouse, turn left, then at once right so the hedge is now on the right. Drop down the hill to a corner gap on to a drive. At once leave the drive, which turns sharp right. Go through a hedge gap into a field. Turn right to walk alongside a right-hand hedge to go over a bridge in the field corner. Turn left. Descend the hill (with a left-hand hedge). At the bottom of the hill turn right. Walk with trees (which hide a brook) on the left to pass through a corner metal gate. In the next pasture, keep on the same heading to a stile beside a gate on to a lane. Turn left to a T-junction. Go right and follow the lane past the church. At another T-junction the Red Lion is to the right.

For the longer walk, keep ahead at the barn, to pass an old house (on the left) called Wheelbarrow Castle and proceed to a lane. Turn right and descend the hill to Little Compton and the pub. This longer walk follows a quiet road and maintains height and views for some distance.